Child
of the
Heart

By Bonnie Willemssen

Bonnie Willemssen

Table of Contents

Acknowledgements

I need to thank so many people for their help and influence on the completion of this book. So many thanks to my friend Ron Amey for digitizing all the corresponding photos and not making me learn how to do it. Thank you to Rob and Debbie O'Byrne for making this a quality piece with their editing and artwork (www.jetlaunch.net). There is no way I would have completed this book without the unwavering support of my friend and first editor—Pat Poehling—who had to slug through all my initial drafts. I can't imagine how I could have bridged the gap from America to Germany without the help of my search consultant, Leonie Boehmer. I am still grateful and amazed at how willingly my siblings accepted me into their lives, especially my brother, Dieter Paul. I never would have searched for my birth family if my daughter, Ann, hadn't encouraged me. To my husband, Jim, thank you for your steadfast patience and support. My parents, Mary and Mark Spettel, need special thanks, postmortem, for adopting me, raising me, and giving me stability. A thank you to Dorothy, the first women who adopted me, for knowing it was the right decision to give me up. And, of course, I'm grateful to my birth parents, Erika and Gerhard, for giving me life.

Prologue

That Little German Girl

When you are young—four or five—there are always adults talking above your head. This was true for me. I would be running errands with my mother, or we would be in church or picnicking in the park, and Mother would run into someone she knew. The first words out of their mouths would be, "Is that the little German girl you adopted?" I'm sure my mother must have hated to keep hearing that, but her upbringing only allowed her to respond in the polite affirmative. "Yes, this is the little girl we chose."

Fifty years later I was helping my husband and his father investigate independent care facilities. As we were visiting one center, I noticed an old friend of my mother's resided there. I stepped in and said hello, introducing myself as Mary Spettel's daughter, Bonnie. She had a couple friends visiting, so I only stayed a minute. As I left, I heard her tell her companions, "That's the little German girl Mary and Mark Spettel adopted."

At that moment I decided that if I ever wrote about the experiences of finding my birth family, I'd call my book *That Little German Girl*. Well, since then there has been a lot of *The*, *Little*, and *Girl* in a whole bunch of other popular books. No way could I use that title. For the last few years I

1

tried to come up with something new, and as you obviously noticed when you picked up this book, it's *Child Of The Heart*. My adoptive mother Mary loved this poem.

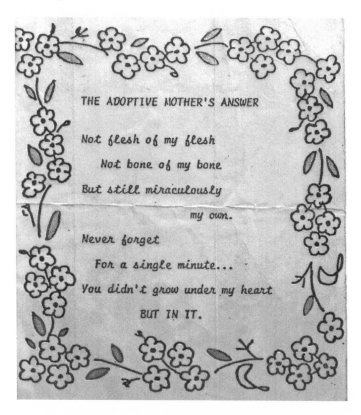

THE ADOPTIVE MOTHER'S ANSWER

Not flesh of my flesh

Not bone of my bone

But still miraculously

my own.

Never forget

For a single minute...

You didn't grow under my heart

BUT IN IT.

I've had seven different names. Was I running from the law? Was I a spy? Nope, just someone given one name at birth. After being adopted twice, though, I accumulated a bunch more. Family and friends were fascinated that I had been born in Germany and that there might be some mysterious family waiting for word of my location.

My best friend and I were having lunch when the topic turned to my heritage. For years we had fun constructing a fantasy family for me. We were sure I was descended from royalty and that they were looking for me. Obviously, it was time for me to ascend to the throne. Never mind that there was no royalty in Germany. I wondered about the mystery of my birth since I was old enough to understand what my adoptive mother meant when she told me, "We chose you."

My adoption was not through an agency. In fact, there was a time when just *taking* me unofficially had been suggested to my second adoptive parents. I did have a "legal" birth certificate formatted by a judge at the time of my adoption so that I would be able to function in the American melting pot that was my new home. I also had the stories my mother and father told me, and wrote about how they met me and almost lost me.

In sixth grade, my desire to know more about my roots and my birth family surfaced big time. I knew there was information in my mother's bedroom desk. So, I searched for and found the key that opened the locked drawer. I found letters from and pictures of my first adoptive mother. I already knew her name—Dorothy. I knew the general story, but I eagerly read the letters in the drawer.

Not everything made sense.

I had been led to believe that my first adoptive mother, Dorothy, could not keep me because she was divorced and in financial trouble. On the back of her picture she had written, "When you show this picture to Bonnie, does she remember me?" I knew I had never seen that picture, ever.

Several years passed and I got curious again. I didn't always get along with my too-old parents (they were 46 and 50 when I was born). To me they were out-of-date and out-of-step compared to my friends' parents. When I was a freshman in high school I went to the secret drawer in my mom's desk again. This time I copied her address and wrote a letter to Dorothy. I told her about my life and asked her what she could tell me about my birth family.

I wanted so badly to know if I had siblings. I asked her to send a reply to my friend's address so my parents would not find out. I felt like I was betraying them by being curious about my birth family. I always wondered if I had a brother or a sister, which at the time sounded like the best thing ever. I had daydreams of the doorbell ringing. I would answer it and there would be my brother, come to claim me, saying that there had been a huge mix-up and they had been looking for me ever since I disappeared—and they wanted me back. *The truth was even more unique.*

Dorothy wrote back to me, sending it to my friend's house. The letter was both sides of four pages with very tight handwriting. My friend brought it to me at school and I thought I would die while I waited for classes to end so I could read it. After the last class, she and I walked to a local department store, pretending to shop. I went into the restroom and read the letter in a stall.

I read it fast. I read it twice. I was disappointed. Dorothy did not know much about my birth family. She only talked about my life with *her*. I was not interested in that. I wish so much that I had kept that letter! But I didn't. After I read it, I tore it into little pieces and flushed it down the toilet. All I took away from it was a glimmer of information about my birth family.

Dorothy thought my birth mother might have had an affair, and was pretty sure that my birth mother's husband was not my father. She also thought I had older half-siblings. The rest of the letter was about living and traveling with her in Germany, France, and Switzerland while she worked in the medical field for the U.S. Army. She asked me to write to her again, but I never did.

Over the years, when I went to a doctor, there would be that inevitable questionnaire about family history and I would put an X through it. I didn't know anything about my medical history. When our first child died within hours of his birth, there was much speculation about my medical background. To their credit, Mary and Mark wanted to find my birth family and tried contacting Dorothy only to learn that she had passed away. In the meantime, the genetic tests said our son's birth defects were not inherited. The matter of my medical history was dropped.

Still, I wondered where I could even start a search for family behind the Iron Curtain. I wished I spoke fluent German, but from the time they adopted me Mary and Mark feared I would carry a stigma if I had even a hint of a German accent. That was 1952 post-WWII America. In La Crosse, Wisconsin, my new hometown, officials renamed Berlin Street because of animosity toward Germany. I took German classes in high school thinking I'd have a knack for the language, but I never accomplished fluid conversation.

"One of these days," I told myself, "I'm going to find my birth family." Part of my foot-dragging was that I didn't want to hurt my adoptive parents. I wasn't sure if our relationship was strong enough to endure such *enlightenment*. Also, there had been no formal adoption agency for me to check to even start my search.

My excuses were always: *When I'm not working; when my daughter doesn't need me; when I have time; when I can speak German better; when the Berlin Wall comes down; and more importantly, when I can handle the knowledge that my birth mother and father are dead and not searching for me or waiting for me to find them. Not looking, not knowing, kept them alive and waiting for me to find them.*

Chapter One

Who am I?

I'm the girl with a lot of names—seven to be exact. There might be more, but who's counting? You probably would like to know why I have so many different names.

I was born Gerda Erika Paul. My birth mother, Erika Gerda Irene (Müller) Paul was 34 when I was born. I was the youngest of six children. My birth father, nine years older than she, was Gerhard Benno Hermann Paul. He was 43 when I came into the world. Apparently, and this is surmised by guesses, family stories, and logic, they did not want another mouth to feed. Gerhard perhaps because he did not believe I was his child, and Erika possibly because she was not sure who my father was either.

By the next month, I belonged to someone else. Dorothy, an American citizen, adopted me. I started with Gerda Erika Elliot but became Mary Christianne Susanne Elliot by the time I was baptized a month later. My godfather was listed as her grown son and my godmother was a woman named Christianne. I was baptized in McNair Barracks Chapel in Berlin, Germany, in the rite of the Roman Catholic Church. According to my passport, I traveled with Dorothy (and a nurse named Clara who later married Dorothy's son) for the next four years in Germany, France and Switzerland. Dorothy was in the military and her job was to help eradicate TB in Europe. With bits and pieces from later discoveries, I have surmised that she had a daughter who died at eight years of age. Perhaps I was a replacement for her.

In 1952, when I was four, Dorothy, my nurse, and a doctor who was a work partner of Dorothy's and I traveled on the return maiden voyage of the *SS United States* to New York City. On this trip, we were seated with an older, childless couple named Mary and Mark Spettel—eventually to become my next parents.

Well, that's the long and the short of it, and if that whets your curiosity, read on, because it's quite a story.

Here is where I'm putting a timeline—it might help you, as it did me, keep it all straight.

April 25, 1876—Hermann Paul, my paternal grandfather, is born.

October 1893—Franz August Müller, my maternal grandfather, is born.

August 29, 1894—Anna (Anni) Schultz Müller, my maternal grandmother, is born

September 1, 1898—Mark J. Spettel, my adopted father, is born.

June 3, 1903—Mary J (Singer) Spettel, my second adopted mother, is born.

October 15, 1905—Gerhard Benno Hermann Paul, my birth father, is born.

October 31, 1914—Erika Gerda Irene (Müller) Paul, my birth mother, is born.

April 13, 1924—Clara, my nurse/nanny, is born.

June 25, 1925—Mary (Singer) and Mark Spettel, my adopted parents, married.

April 7, 1934—Erika Müller and Gerhard Paul, my birth parents, are married.

July 19, 1934—Helga Paul, my sister, is born (and yes, my birth mother was pregnant before she was married).

October 8, 1936—Klaus Paul, my brother, is born.

April 16, 1939—Dietrich (Dieter) Paul, my brother, is born.

April 5, 1943—Detlaf (Detti) Paul, my brother, is born.

August 8, 1945—Rainer Paul, my brother, is born.

September 9, 1945—Rainer Paul dies.

November 5, 1946—Erika and Gerhard, my birth parents, divorce.

June 5, 1948—Erika and Gerhard, my birth parents, remarry, and she is pregnant with me.

July 30, 1948—Gerda Erika Paul (me) is born in a hospital in Lichtenberg, Germany.

September 1, 1948—I am baptized as Mary Christianne Susanne Elliot.

June 13, 1951—Agreement between Erika and Gerard Paul, my birth parents, and Dorothy, my first adoptive mother, was finalized for me.

March 10, 1952—Jean Lusk's funeral.

June 1952—Bonnie (a nickname that was never on any official paperwork) and Dorothy travel to the United States.

September 1952—Dorothy asks Mary and Mark Spettel to "watch" Bonnie while she travels back to Germany for a "short trip."

November 9, 1953—Mary Christianne Susanne officially becomes Mary Jean Spettel.

November 8, 1956—Mary Susan Spettel becomes a naturalized citizen, dropping the middle name Jean.

June 1962—Mary, Mark and Bonnie Spettel travel to Europe and Berlin, Germany. Bonnie and Mary travel on a dual passport that does not reveal where Bonnie was born.

June 19, 1966—Mary and Mark request a "legal" birth certificate so I can travel to Mexico.

February 6, 1970—my birth parents make a will, excluding their son, Klaus, from any inheritance. It does not mention me.

April 29, 1972—Mary Susan Spettel marries James Henry Willemssen and becomes Mary Susan Willemssen.

1972—Helga Paul, my sister, is divorced.

February 28, 1977—Erik Michael Willemssen, first child of Bonnie and Jim, is born and dies the same day.

1977—Erika Paul, my birth mother, has her first occurrence of breast cancer.

May 15, 1977—Ramona Paul, my brother Dieter's only child, is born.

December 27, 1977—Gerhard, my birth father, dies at age 73.

November 16, 1978—Ann Elizabeth Willemssen, our daughter, is born.

1982—Breast cancer returns for Erika, my birth mother.

November 11, 1983—Erika Gerda Irene (Müller) Paul, my birth mother, dies at age 70.

May 27, 1986—I change my name legally from Mary Susan Willemssen to Bonnie Ann Willemssen.

1989—Berlin Wall comes down.

November 13, 1990—Mark J. Spettel, my adoptive father, dies at age 92.

1991—Dieter finds Klaus but cannot find me, his younger sister.

1992—Dieter and his family travel to the U.S. for the first time.

April 25, 1999—first email to Leonie Boehmer, a search consultant for German-born adoptees.

April 27, 2000—Dieter Paul, my brother, and Helga Stademann, my sister, call me. We hear each other's voices for the very first time ever.

September 5, 2000—I meet my three brothers and my sister for the first time in my 52 years. I also meet my niece, Ramona, at the airport, and my sister-in-law, Eszter, at their apartment later that morning.

October 25, 2000—DNA testing for paternity between Dieter and myself. Almost 100% proof that we share the same mother *and* the same father.

April 20, 2001—Helga is the first to visit me in America.

August 2001—Ramona comes to La Crosse, WI for 5 weeks.

October 6, 2001—Mary Josephine (Singer) Spettel, my second adoptive mother, dies at age 98.

July 2002—Dieter, Ramona and Eszter come to La Crosse for a visit.

Summer, 2003—Jim and I go to Germany to visit.

April 6, 2005—Detti, my brother, dies at 60 years and one day.

Summer, 2006—Ann and I go to Germany to visit.

December 3, 2007—Helga, my sister, dies at age 74.

May 15, 2008—Clara, my nanny, dies at 84.

July 11, 2013—My godfather, the son of my first adopted mother and the husband of my nurse/nanny, dies.

June 1, 2016—Klaus, my brother, dies at age 80.

Chapter Two

Not a Large-Scale Event

In 1932 FDR won the presidential race in the United States, but Erika Müller didn't think much about that at the tender age of 18. Dashiell Hammet wrote *The Thin Man,* but she would never read it. Heartthrob Gary Cooper played the lead in *A Farewell to Arms,* but it would not reach Germany for several years. Hermann Wilhelm Goring was elected Speaker of the Reichstag, but why would a young girl in her late teens care about that? Charles Lindberg's baby was kidnapped and the world was shocked. Einstein placed the earth's age at 10 billion years and she felt a fleeting pride for her countryman's intellect, but Erika neither wanted nor needed to be inspired by this news.

Erika had more important things to think of on that warm August day in 1932 because she was going dancing at the *Tanzenhalle* that night with her first cousin and best friend, Sophie.

Erika and Sophie always arrived exactly at 6:00, before the good tables were taken. They liked to be close to the dance floor so they would be noticed. That afternoon had been lazy and sweltering, but Erika knew that when any boys asked, she would dance with abandon. She was happy and filled with the desire to enjoy life. Her beauty and a helpless "take care of me" attitude appealed to many.

All week she had thought of what she would wear—her skirt with the cabbage roses on it and the silk blouse that Mama had found in the thrift shop. Her shoes, worn many times, were polished. She was lucky that hose was too expensive for most of the girls; they would all go without and everyone would blame the heat. She twisted her blond hair behind her head and fastened it low on her slender neck in the style of the time. She wanted to be accepted by the other *Madchen* (girls) that would be crowding into the large hall. The cousins, so close in age they could have been twins, sat twisting their drinks in nervous hands, hoping to be asked to dance.

"*Fraulein?*" he asked. Erika slowly looked up, wondering who was speaking. He was looking at her. Erika had never seen this man before, and he was a man, most definitely, and older by many years than the young, skinny, anxious boys who frequented the dance hall. Her heart fluttered. In her inexperienced eyes he was handsome and sophisticated, especially in his German army uniform. Sophie giggled and pushed her arm, encouraging her. As Erika stood, she blushed, but told him she would very much enjoy dancing with him. He took her in his arms and they danced a foxtrot to *Auf Einem Regenbogen,* and *I'm Dancing in a Rainbow* became their song. It was rhythmic and romantic, and she melted in his arms, her skin flushing at his touch. She fell in love during this dance, at this time, with this man.

His name was Gerhard. It was the beginning—my mother and father meeting in a dance hall in Berlin, Germany. It was the start of a two-year courtship that resulted in a marriage that produced six children, the youngest being me. It is the story of wars and walls, separations and reunions, tensions and tears.

The ballroom where my birth parents met.

Erika (my birth mother) at 18, with Gerhard (my birth father) at 29. Before their marriage.

Chapter Three

April 27, 2000

It was a chilly spring morning, the kind of morning where you dig deeper under the covers rather than get up and close the window. I was jolted awake by the ringing phone. There were only two reasons someone would call me at 5:30 a.m.—my mom in the nursing home had died or my daughter had an emergency at college. To my hesitant hello there was an equally hesitant voice asking, "Is this Bonnie Willemssen?"

"Yes," I said, confused by the heavy accent. His next five words sent shock waves through me.

"This is your brother, Dieter."

On one level I knew what was happening. My letter had reached Germany. I could hear myself saying, "Oh my God, oh my God," over and over. My husband was alarmed at first but could see that I was excited, not sad. I was afraid to move a muscle for fear the connection would break. I was speaking with my brother and yet I had never heard his voice in my entire life.

He said they had received my letter and that he had searched for me for years. I pressed the phone as close to my ear as I could. His English was halting and obviously not easy for him. He said, "If we speak slowly, we will be able to understand each other." I listened, interjecting only when it seemed appropriate. *What do you say during your first phone call with a sibling you didn't know existed until a few months ago? Who is the Helga I wrote to in my letter? How did our mother die? Did my siblings want to meet me?*

As my thoughts swirled, my brother explained that his sister—*our sister?*—Helga, had received my letter the day before. It was the letter where I introduced myself, sent a picture of me with my daughter and my husband, and also a copy of my birth certificate and a copy of a letter her father—*our father?*—had written giving me up for adoption. After reading the letter, shocked and excited, she called Dieter. He drove right over to her apartment and they figured out the time in Wisconsin, and then sat and waited for a "decent" time to call me. And that time was 5:30 in the morning on Thursday, April 27, 2000.

So, the year 2000 turned out to be pretty good for me. No Y2K, no end of the world, no global economic collapse—just four living siblings finding each other.

My sister did not speak a single word of English, but later in the conversation, Dieter said she wanted to try to speak to me. I attempted a few words of high school German. Her words tumbled out in a jumble of sounds and syllables and the sniffing back of tears. I didn't understand anything she said. But, I had just heard the voices of my brother and my sister. And apparently, I had two more brothers who were still alive.

Dieter told me that he was the only one who knew my mother had had a sixth child. When she died in 1983 he had gone through the family bible and found my name and birth date listed. There had been a baby boy born three years before me who only lived a few months. His death certificate was included, but nothing for me, the sixth child. Dieter went to the appropriate government offices to get a copy of my *death* certificate so he could update the bible, and there he discovered that I had been adopted. He said he could not do much else at the time because he and the rest of my birth family lived behind the Iron Curtain.

I was born in the summer of 1948 in Berlin, Germany. At the time of my birth, the war had divided Berlin into four sectors. My family lived in the borough of Lichtenberg, which was given to the Soviet Union. My mother, Erika, gave me up for adoption immediately after my birth. Two months later I was baptized with a different name. By 1955 I again had a new name, when I was adopted a second time.

This is the story of my life…of having three mothers, of finding three brothers and a sister. It is a 50-year mystery interlaced with lies, deceit, heartache, and joy.

Chapter Four

2000—A German Family

Dieter and I spoke for an hour on the phone that morning in April. I clutched the receiver so tightly my hand ached. *What if the connection was broken? How could I call him back?* He told me about trying to find me. *He was trying to find me?* He didn't know what to do after the roadblock he encountered in 1983 while tracing me. He decided to never tell his siblings that I existed because he was unsuccessful in his quest.

In 1989 the Berlin Wall came down and in 1990 Dieter again tried to search for me. He asked for help from the Red Cross. He followed "my trail" over the four years from my birth in 1948 until I left Germany in 1952. Unbelievable as it might sound, he is convinced that my second mother and I lived in the *same apartment building* as my birth mother and my siblings. Then he said something that filled my heart with joy. He said, "*We have been waiting for you.*"

I learned that my siblings were all older than I. Helga, the first girl, was 16 when I was born. After we met, and I got to know her a little better, I asked her if it was possible I was *her* child and that Erika just pretended to be my mother. My niece had to be our verbal go-between, but Helga insisted that was not the case and Klaus, only a year younger, said he knew that was not true. He and Helga both remembered their mother—*our mother*—being pregnant, yet not coming home from the hospital with a baby. Dieter (short for Dietrich) was next in birth order at nine years older than I, and Detti (a nickname for Detlaf) was closest to my age at five years older. Ran died as an infant.

After I located them, Dieter went back to the government offices for more information, and there he discovered some facts about our mother and father and the time frame surrounding my birth that surprised him.

I had written in my initial contact letter that I was sure that "our" mother had an affair and that I was a half-sister. Dieter said, in that first call, "*We are not half-brothers and sister, we are whole.*" I let that statement go, thinking, *why else would she give me up?*

In my contact letter, I had asked if they had any medical information that I could pass along to my daughter and Dieter told me our mother had died of breast cancer. That alone was worth the effort of my long search. Dieter said that his father, Gerhard, had died of colon cancer, but sad as that was for them, it didn't mean much to me because he was not my father. Or so I thought.

I was speaking to this person, this blood relative, my brother, for the very first time in my life. Being raised as an only child meant I missed out on having siblings. *Did my birth mother ever think of me? Did she care at all?* I asked Dieter if she had ever said anything about me. He said she had gone to her grave never mentioning having given up a baby for adoption. He thought maybe she was embarrassed, and I interpreted that to mean because she had had an affair. Later, as different facts came to light, we decided that she was embarrassed that she had given me away at all.

After we hung up I tried to tell my husband everything I learned, but I was so excited that I just talked in circles. I decided I had to sit down and write as much of our conversation as I could remember. In Wisconsin it was 6:30 a.m. and I called my daughter who was attending Oberlin College in Ohio where it was 7:30. I cannot remember what details I told her. I was crying and laughing, blowing my nose, and talking a mile a minute, but I do remember what she said to me. "I'm so happy for *you*, Mom. Now you will know who you are."

My heart was doing weird little flip-flops. My brain was skittering around from thought to thought. I feared that I wouldn't be able to figure out how to call my brother back using the phone numbers he had given me. I wished I didn't have to wait until the next week to call, but we had agreed on the following Thursday.

Those next six days were a long wait. I spent the time telling everyone I knew in the world about my phone call with my brother. They all shared my excitement but no one, unless they had lived my life, knew what I was feeling. A connection with family—birth family—people who might look like me and walk like me and sound like me. What in the world would it be like to meet them in person?

My birth family in 1944. Mama and
Papa, Klaus, Detti, Dieter, Helga….
two missing – Rainer and Gerda (me).

Chapter Five

Under the Clothesline

Erika met Dorothy in the summer of 1947 under the clotheslines in the backyard of their apartment building in East Germany. They never dreamed that they would one day be two mothers sharing one child. They started their friendship as most women do, exchanging pleasantries, commenting on the warm weather, and complaining about the economic status of Germany since the end of the war.

Erika, always surrounded by children, cooled herself on the peeling old bench in the shade of the forty-foot-tall oaks. She had just finished hanging the family's laundry on her line; each apartment was allowed one line for hanging clothes. No one owned such a treasure as a washing machine, so she did the wash in the big tub in the washroom shared by everyone. The family had only recently moved to this crumbling apartment building from a nicer place in Berlin because circumstances were deteriorating for Erika. Her husband, Gerhard, a prisoner of war in France for several years, had returned to Berlin, but unable to overcome his disillusionment and anger with how life turned out for him, had divorced his younger wife and left for Bavaria to seek employment and companionship elsewhere.

He visited the children now and then, leaving a little money for their care. Sometimes he would linger, acting as if he was interested in staying, but then he would go again. Erika was never sure if he would come back, nor if she wanted him to.

Erika found other ways to fill her days—and nights. She was only 33, and with four children to feed and clothe, she needed to make ends meet. She found Alfred, or rather he found her, through an ad she had placed at the local market looking for someone to rent one of the sleeping rooms. He was part of the Inter-Allied Control Council, a representative of the newly-formed Free Democratic Party in Germany. He would be in the Eastern sector for only a few months and needed temporary living quarters, which were hard to find because so many buildings had been reduced to rubble during the war. He had found her ad and she had found someone to help pay the bills. By day he fought for his ideals, and by night he quietly assimilated himself into Erika's family and her life.

Shortly, happily, he found himself sharing her bed and soon the children accepted him as the man of the house. When her husband made his infrequent visits, Alfred made himself scarce. He wondered, but never asked, where Gerhard slept during those visits.

As days became shorter and nights became chilly, Erika cried on Dorothy's shoulder, sharing her deep, dark secret. She was pregnant. She was distraught. Financially, she could hardly afford to feed the five of them, and just last month Alfred had been reassigned to Munich, a promotion for him and a stab in the heart for her. Another renter had not stepped forward, and with winter coming, she was worried about fuel as well as food. What should she do?

Together they formulated a plan. Erika would write to Gerhard and tell him she was pregnant, never suggesting that she questioned the paternity. She would beg him to return to her and his children. She worried about his frequent rages, but when her letter found him in the south, he did return to them and things seemed like they would work out. She didn't plan on the children talking so much about Alfred—how fun he was; how he helped them with their homework and brought little treats for them; how Mama laughed and laughed with him. Gerhard soon realized that Alfred was more than a renter. He confronted her, called her a cheating wife, and she reminded him that they were still divorced.

Gerhard was a hard and determined man, and he delivered an ultimatum. He would only stay with her and the other four children, *his* children, if she gave this child—the one in her belly—up for adoption. He said he would not claim the child as his. Erika accepted the decision. They would marry again, they would be a family again, and they would never speak of it again. In the months that followed Gerhard's return to the household, things went better. Money was more plentiful because Gerhard had found a job as a taxi driver, and with so many diplomats in town he was kept busy.

The spring of 1948 was welcomed by Erika and Dorothy because they would have the opportunity to chat again under the clotheslines. It was on such a day that Dorothy suggested to Erika that she give the baby to her. Dorothy, a US Army nurse, was estranged from her German-born husband and had lost a child to tuberculosis several years earlier. She pointed out that Erika could watch the child grow up right there in the apartment complex they shared. Erika seized on that idea. She could appease her husband and still have her child, but how to do it without Gerhard knowing? Although she knew that Gerhard did not care where Erika had the baby, or who took it, she was sure he would not approve of Dorothy's idea.

So, she kept another secret. On June 30th, Gerhard and Erika remarried and on July 30th, it was Dorothy who helped Erika on the bus and to the hospital to have her little girl. When Erika returned without a baby, the older children did not ask any questions. Erika had already lost one child to crib death several years earlier and they remembered her tears and sadness. They did not want to upset her again. Soon they realized that Mama was very happy. Dorothy, their neighbor and Mama's good friend, had a new baby, and Mama loved to be over at her apartment all the time. Dorothy called the baby Bonnie, but Mama couldn't seem to remember that, and called her Gerda. Interestingly, that was Mama's middle name.

This is a possible scenario between two women—one my birth mother, and one my first adoptive mother—of how I was "passed" from Erika to Dorothy.

They shared a secret and a child. Me. My name changed from Gerda Erika Paul—the name on my birth certificate on July 30, 1948—to Mary Christianne Suzanne Elliott, the name on my baptismal certificate on September 1, 1948. There are no records, but I used anecdotes from the stories I learned from my family when I found them to write this chapter. All I do know is that my birth mother went to her grave mute on the subject of me.

I am standing outside the apartment building that my birth family lived in when I was born. Perhaps I lived there at the same time with my adoptive mother.

Chapter Six

2000—The Second Phone Call

During our first phone call from my brother, there had been a mix-up in language. Dieter tried to tell me his daughter, Ramona, who could speak English, was going to be home on Tuesday (*Dienstag*), but I misunderstood and thought he said Thursday (*Donnerstad*). It was torture to wait a whole week, but I thought that was what he wanted me to do. I was so afraid that our thin thread of a connection was going to be lost forever. I had found them. I didn't want to lose them. While I waited for the week to pass, I had our telephone company hook us up with long-distance to Germany. It was the only way I knew of at the time to make long-distance calls.

Thursday finally came, and I called. I was new to calling Germany and made several dialing mistakes before I got it right. Today it's "old hat" to call them. Ramona answered on the first ring and introduced herself as my niece. It was so wonderful to speak with someone who spoke English. She told me they had waited all Tuesday evening for me to call. She said they didn't want to call me and seem pushy, but they did think perhaps there was a miscommunication.

When I spoke with Dieter during our first call I was struggling so much to follow the conversation that I hoped I would remember what he was telling me. During the second call I found out so much more, and I took notes. I asked Ramona if I looked like her dad. She said yes, but that I looked a whole lot like her. I had only sent one picture of Jim, Ann and me. Ramona was very excited to learn she had an aunt in the United States and a female first cousin only one year younger. How I wish the girls could have known each other when they were younger.

From then until Labor Day there were hundreds of contacts made between my siblings and me. We emailed, we chatted on the phone, we wrote. We sent gifts to each other. I learned that Dieter had worked for the East German airlines before the Wall of Shame (Dieter's name for it) was torn down. Luckily, he was able to get a job with Lufthansa, but at less pay and the loss of all his seniority and pension that he had built to that point. One wonderful perk he did have though was that the three of them could travel anywhere in the world for free and also enjoy the many discounts for Lufthansa employees at hotels and resorts.

Again, as with the first phone call, I was glued to the receiver, hoping not to miss a word. Ramona told me Helga had married and moved with her new husband into what would two weeks later become the West Sector of Berlin. Now she was retired from a job with the license bureau and had a good pension. She never had any children and her husband passed away after they divorced.

My brother, Detti, had been married four times and had five kids. My new niece confessed that no one was exactly sure how many children or marriages Detti had had. He, like Dieter and the rest of the family, lived through the occupation of the Eastern sector of Berlin. Detti was a house painter when he wasn't drinking. He currently lived with a woman named Rosie in her apartment. Dieter said he and Dieter were currently not speaking because of a disagreement five years earlier. At the time of our phone call, no one had told Detti or Klaus about me.

My niece attended Humboldt University, majoring in business, and was living at home to save money. She sounded like a very smart young lady. Thank God she had email. It made all the difference in the world for communication with my new family. Her first email to me was on May 3, 2000. At this point, we had already spoken numerous times on the phone.

I forwarded all the emails to my daughter, Ann, so she would know all the particulars as I learned about them.

My sister made her first of many calls to me at 5 p.m. my time (very late her time). I was nervous. It's hard to have a conversation when you don't understand what is being said. I was perspiring by the end of our first ten-minute call. I could hear the frustration in her voice that I didn't understand what she was trying to say. The four of them, my siblings, had never learned English in school. They grew up in the East sector and learned Russian as their second language.

Dieter learned some English working for the airlines and by teaching himself. My brother Klaus lived in Frankfurt from his late teens. He had run away from home at 17 and learned his limited English from transporting tourists during his various jobs, including driving a limo. Detti, and especially Helga, had no interest in learning English.

Over the next few months we kept the post office in business. Letters flew back and forth, most accompanied by pictures or copies of pictures. A big problem was that I was writing in English and they were writing in German. My brother Dieter knew some English and he did a fair job of making himself understood when we spoke.

I was in Seventh Heaven. Can you imagine anything more exciting than learning about your long-lost siblings and your roots? Suddenly my German heritage was front and center. Over the years I rarely mentioned being born in Germany unless it was necessary. I was an American. But now, I was slipping into the past. I was morphing into That Little German Girl whom everyone in my hometown knew about when I was first adopted.

Chapter Seven

1952—Cruise of Destiny

It was June of 1952, and a young German girl named Bonnie was getting ready to board a massive ship with her *Mutti*, Dorothy. The name of the ship, stenciled on the side, was the *SS United States*. Those words meant nothing to the little girl, but to her mother, they meant the possibility of reconciliation with the American family she had abandoned many years before.

She was divorced from her husband. Her war work with the Army was dwindling and she wanted to make an effort to reunite with her family in Delaware. She traveled with a doctor that she worked with, and Bonnie, the child she had adopted four years earlier in Berlin. The three of them and a nanny named Clara had boarded the ship as early as possible so they could get unpacked and settled. Immediately, Dorothy availed herself of the nursery on board the ship so she could unpack and rest.

Earlier that year, in January, snow covered the lawns and temperatures dropped to 17 degrees below zero in La Crosse, Wisconsin. There were some nice days too, into the upper 40s, and those days helped Mary and

Mark make it through yet another dreary winter, working hard at the office supply store they owned and operated.

A bright spot in their lives was Jean. She started as a clerk, friendly and capable. She grew to be their friend and pseudo daughter; the child Mary could never have. Jean was 21 that winter and had just become engaged to Dale, a local boy. They were madly in love, spending every free moment together, and Mary and Mark were happy for the young couple.

The red spots appeared on Jean's cheeks in early February. Mary commented on them, but Jean assured her it was frostbite from her many nights of ice skating on the lagoon with Dale.

Mary remembered her girlhood of holding hands and skating 'round and 'round the rink with Mark at her side. The future seemed so bright. At that time, Mark was to go to the University in Madison to become a lawyer and she was taking classes to become a stenographer. But after only one year, life intervened. Mark's father died and Mark returned to La Crosse to take over the family grocery store. Mary worked for several years for a local law office. Eventually, they sold the grocery business and Mark got a position clerking at an office supply store. Later he would become its competitor.

By February Jean could no longer ignore the spots on her cheeks. A trip to Mayo Clinic in Rochester, Minnesota, revealed she had leukemia. The diagnosis was devastating to both couples, young and old. Jean's illness progressed quickly. At each visit from the older couple, Jean would beg Mary not to postpone their trip to Europe planned for that summer. It was to be their first trip abroad and plans had been in motion for many months. Just getting Mark to agree to take a trip was a hurdle, his dedication to his store absolute. Mary's tears were the only answer. The trip would be postponed. But Jean begged again and again and, finally, Mary relented, her heart breaking for Jean who cared so much for her "pseudo-parents."

By March, Jean was gone and in June of 1952, Mary and Mark departed to begin their trip, hearts filled with bittersweet joy for the adventure ahead and sadness behind.

Right before their first cruise, Mary and Mark learned that the *SS United States* was leaving France to make the return portion of her maiden voyage. Mary wanted to be on it. With an ease that could only happen back in that era, Mary was able to make the switch from one cruise ship to another for the return voyage. The *SS United States* was built as the fastest ship of the time. Fire was the greatest fear onboard ocean-going vessels, so the owners had built it entirely out of aluminum. No wood was used in the ship's framing, accessories, decorating, or interior surfaces to minimize the risk of fire. Even the grand piano was to be made of aluminum, but someone discovered they could make it of a rare, fire-resistant wood. The piano was accepted only after it was tested by pouring gasoline upon the wood and igniting it. The wood did not burn.

The trip was enlightening. It was wonderful to see the places Mary's sister, Betty, had boasted of seeing. Betty and her husband, Frank, had made several trips across the seas before Mary and Mark had even flown on a plane. The world travelers always brought home exotic items, purchased on continents whose names Mary and Mark knew from the globe, and each object was given a place of honor in their house. On each outbound trip for Mary's sister and her husband, Mary and Mark would drive the older couple to the airport. Weeks later they would pick them up, listening to stories of their adventures on the ride home and over dinner the next night. Tending to Betty's various pets and household plants was a role Mary accepted willingly, as her sister lived a life Mary could only dream about.

The anticipated day came at last to return home on the new *SS United States*. Their wonderful trip was almost over. Only the cruise home stood between them and reality. Four days left of fine food, staff to cater to them, and strolls along the promenade. Mark and Mary had heard the chatter about the ship's world speed record, beating the *Queen Mary* by ten hours from NYC to France. They could board in the early afternoon and were excited to see the whole ship right away.

Before luggage had even been transferred to their cabin, they were eagerly comparing the brand-new ship to the elegant and stately *Queen Mary*. On one deck they noticed the nursery. Peeking in, they saw children already playing there. A little girl of about four ran up to the Dutch door, which was locked at the bottom and open at the top, and began chatting with them in German. It was not unusual for passengers of every nationality to be traveling in those days. The war was over, and people were feeling the hope of better times ahead. Many people used the safer but slower passage of the ships to get to and from Europe. The little girl with blond curls and hazel eyes, seeing that her words were not understood, motioned for them to enter. Mary and Mark smiled and shook their heads. No one was allowed to enter the nursery except parents. Even in those days, people were mistrustful of strangers.

Mary and Mark finished their exploration and went to their cabin to unpack, freshen up, and proceed to the dining room for the first meal. They wondered who their tablemates might be. They originally had a table for two reserved but decided it would be fun to chat with other people. The request had been made to the *maître d'*, and he agreed to seat them at a larger table.

They entered the gorgeous room and stood at the top of a short flight of stairs, staring in wonderment at the beauty of the crystal chandeliers reflected in the crystal goblets set on the tables in anticipation of the diners for the 5 o'clock seating. Mark suggested the earlier dinner time so they could see the nightly show and then retire early. They were exhausted from three weeks of touring city after city, and once they got home they needed to return to their early-rising work days.

They were escorted to the table. Already seated was a tall, dark-haired woman in her early 40s and an equally tall, distinguished man. Next to the woman was a much younger girl and seated next to her was a child. They were surprised to see it was the little girl from the nursery. Mary and Mark were thrilled. How fun to have a child to entertain them. The woman introduced herself as Dorothy and said her male companion, a doctor, was head of a TB sanatorium in southern Germany near the Swiss border.

The young woman was the nanny, Clara, and the child was called Bonnie. They discovered that the nanny and the child spoke no English, but Dorothy was an American who had been living in Berlin for years. Her constant travels required a nanny. The doctor, who was not her husband, was accompanying them to New York for reasons that were unclear. It seemed to Mary and Mark that the doctor and Dorothy were more than just acquaintances. They were traveling together *and* sharing the same cabin. No comments were made about that arrangement until Mary and Mark were in private, and then it was discussed in hushed voices, with unflattering judgment on the part of Mary.

The days went by quickly. Mary and Mark looked forward to meal time. Seeing the little German girl and interacting with her was the highlight of their trip. They tried to communicate with her, teaching her a word or two of English, and each night bringing her little gifts that delighted her. The ship sailed, too soon, into New York harbor.

Many on that ship were awestruck to see the Statue of Liberty, but Mary and Mark stood in its shadow with a feeling of sadness. At the last breakfast, they expressed their gratitude for having been placed at the same table with the shipboard strangers and felt a closeness no one would feel in normal circumstances. They offered their help to Dorothy if ever she had to return to Germany for her work, indicating they would "babysit" for the child.

She thanked them for the gesture, but both parties knew it was not to be taken for truth. They exchanged addresses and phone numbers and, too quickly, the ship docked. In the throngs of people departing, they did not see Dorothy, her doctor friend, the nanny, or the little German girl again.

Mary and Mark knew the reality would be pictures exchanged with a Christmas card for a year or two and then nothing. It had been lovely to have a child around, a distraction, always in need of help with cutting meat, or pouring milk, or slipping on a sweater. Mary and Mark acted like grandparents presiding over their small family. Dorothy, either recognizing that they needed to do this, or not caring, didn't interfere.

At the last goodbye, Mary and Mark hugged Bonnie tightly, knowing that she would never remember them; that her life was to be filled with new places and faces. They didn't know the reason for the estrangement Dorothy had with her family. In 1952, people did not share their life stories, at least not in the first few days of acquaintanceship. Hands were shaken with the doctor and Dorothy; the nanny ignored. They gave Bonnie one last hug, and with that, Mary and Mark turned and left. Never in a million years did they anticipate what this chance encounter meant to their future—that the little German girl would someday be their daughter.

Two weeks later, they received a letter from Dorothy. She hinted that things were not going well in Delaware and that Bonnie was not happy in day care. She suggested that perhaps Mary and Mark could take her temporarily while she (Dorothy) got back on her feet. Mary wrote to her on July 30, 1952 (Bonnie's birthday, although she did not know that at the time) that no, they were not interested in taking care of a child. It would disrupt their lives and they were quite busy with their business. Dorothy then called them. She said she needed to go back to Switzerland and could they please just take Bonnie for a month.

Did I feel neglected? Abandoned? Was I hurt that my mother was not around? Did I wonder where she went? How could I ask when I didn't speak any English? I know Mary and Mark tried very hard to make the transition easy and fun and hoping I was fairly settled and content.

Mary and Mark Spettel aboard the SS United States, soon to meet me, their future daughter.

Sailing Home on S.S. United States 1952

Postcard Mary saved from the voyage.

Doctor (travel companion of Dorothy), me, Mark (soon to be my adoptive father) and Dorothy (my first adoptive mother).

The young woman I was briefly named after – Jean Lusk.

Gifts that Mary and Mark gave to me each night at dinner on the ship.

Chapter Eight

August 1952—Two Worlds Meet

Mary was surprised by Dorothy's flightiness. She realized Dorothy remembered how much the Spettels had enjoyed being around Bonnie, and how they had offered to help out if she needed them. Should they help her out for a brief time? A month at most? They had to discuss it.

"What is *wrong* with this woman?" Mary asked over supper.

"Well, maybe it's just like she said, things didn't work out with her family and she couldn't find good child care and she remembered us."

"Who would entrust their child to strangers?"

Mary was frustrated that her husband didn't seem concerned. Instead, he said, "I think it sounds like fun. How hard can it be? It's only a short while." Mark's optimism was the bane of her existence. She wanted life to be organized and practical. He was easy going, humor never more than a chuckle away. After talking for a few days, they agreed that taking care of a four-year-old couldn't be that difficult. It was but a brief diversion from their routine. They assumed, incorrectly, that Bonnie would speak some English after so many months in America, and that communication wouldn't be that difficult.

She called Dorothy. "We'll help you out." It was arranged. Mark couldn't leave his store in the middle of the week, so Mary traveled alone to Chicago, nervous but excited to have a new adventure—a child to care for. As she sat on the train hearing the clacking of the wheels over the tracks, Mary wondered if Bonnie had grown. On the ship, she appeared small for four. Hopefully, Dorothy had taught her some English to help her fit into her new world.

The five hours on the train melted away. Soon she would meet Dorothy and Bonnie at the Palmer House where Mary had called to reserve two rooms. The next day Dorothy would fly back to Delaware, and Bonnie and Mary would get back on the Zephyr to return to Wisconsin.

Mary had been dozing in the luxurious room, waiting, when the phone trilled. It was Dorothy. She and Bonnie had checked into their room, but she had a terrible headache, and would Mary take Bonnie to dinner? With a frown, Mary agreed, and a few minutes later knocked on the door with Bonnie's hand clutched tightly in hers.

Mary led the way to the elevator and down to the formal dining room. It took only a few minutes to discover that Bonnie did not speak a word of English. Mary frowned again, wondering why Dorothy had not tried to teach her at least a few words. The war was over, and German was not a popular language in the United States. No one wanted to admit they had relatives in the old country—not if that old country was Germany. Speculation on who knew what during the incarceration and elimination of Jews was still in people's minds. If she were Dorothy, she would have been making sure Bonnie learned English quickly, and without an accent.

Dinner was good, the waiter attentive, and the little German girl's blond curls bobbed as she chattered in her own language. Conversation was manageable because Mary remembered some German from her Swiss father. Mary tried to teach Bonnie a few words: fork, knife, glass, chicken, rice. Bonnie repeated the words but grew weary and was returned to Dorothy's room for the night. Mary called Mark. It was a great expense to make a long distance phone call, but she just had to share what had transpired so far. Mark said he would be there to meet the train the next day.

When morning arrived, Mary, Dorothy, and Bonnie had breakfast together. Dorothy spoke to Bonnie and Mary thought it seemed like she was telling the child she would be going to the Spettels for a few weeks. Bonnie seemed distressed and frightened. Mary felt sorry for her confusion, thinking Dorothy should have prepared for this moment instead of springing it at the last minute. Still, what did she know? She didn't have children. Maybe it was to save a small child from worrying too soon.

They parted in front of the hotel. The doorman hailed a taxi for Mary and Bonnie to go to Union Station and another for Bonnie's mother to return to the airport. The cab flew through the streets of downtown Chicago to the station, rocking them back and forth in the rear seat. Bonnie was quiet through the ride. Mary did not have the words in German to say what she needed to say to comfort her. Soon they were at the station. Mary held Bonnie's hand again, worried about the large crowd of travelers.

The luggage was portaged to their train car and they settled in their seats. Bonnie seemed eager to sit by the window. Mary felt better seated on the aisle to keep the little girl protected. During the ride, they visited the dining car where Bonnie ate turtle soup and saltine crackers. She loved looking at the brightly colored children's menu with animal characters printed on it. Bonnie did not have anything to play with; not a doll or toy or book. Were they packed in her little suitcase? Luckily, Mary had brought a stuffed pink dachshund (later lost to basement mold) as a little gift. She gave it to Bonnie, who had no idea what to do with it. Mary demonstrated hugging it and tossing it in the air, and Bonnie understood it was to play with. She was distracted by the gift for the rest of the trip.

What could have been going through my mind back then? Did I remember Mary from the ship? Did I wonder where my mother had gone? Did I get frustrated trying to speak to this new person sitting next to me? Was I afraid? I don't know. I don't remember any of it.

And instead of a month, it was one year before Dorothy returned to reclaim Bonnie.

Chapter Nine

1952—First Day in Wisconsin

The train arrived in La Crosse and Mary gathered her sweater and her *Saturday Evening Post* and stepped into the aisle. The porter helped her carry her classy leather suitcase and the small cardboard one with the plastic handle and plastic latch. The child was confused. Mary realized Bonnie didn't know they were disembarking. She leaned over and took the little girl's hand and smiled, hoping that would reassure her better than words spoken in a foreign language.

Mark was so excited. He was looking forward to seeing Bonnie again. A child would be a distraction from work and the monotony of day-to-day life. He was 54 years old, Mary was 50, and they would not be having any children of their own. Over the years, Mary had insinuated herself into her sister Sue's life, helping her raise her five children, even to the point of having the youngest—a girl—live with them on and off while her sister dealt with four boys. That was years ago, and there were no new nieces or nephews to coddle or cuddle.

Mary was the youngest of nine children and never received a lot of attention—no birthday parties, no presents, and no cakes. Raised by a widowed mother, there was neither time nor money for frivolous things. Mark was the younger of two boys both born before the turn of the century, and he was feeling old in 1952. The little girl from the ship would be there only briefly, but something to look forward to nonetheless.

He saw her shoes first: black patent leather with white ankle socks trimmed with lace. Then he saw a small, thin child of four, hazel eyes darting in every direction, fear and anxiety obvious in the pale face. Smooth blond curls reached to below her jawline. He moved to the train steps and reached out to help her maneuver them, but she would have none of that and got off the step without assistance. Mary followed, a smile on her face for her husband.

"I'm so glad we got here in time. I was worried we would be late. I'm eager to get Bonnie home and settled. She needs a long nap, a hot meal, and a good night's rest. Look at her. She doesn't look like she's eaten at all since we last saw her. And those circles under her eyes concern me. Why does she look so tired? I wonder if Dorothy had a consistent bedtime for her. Well, that will change while she's in our care. At least for the month we'll have her."

Mark, leading the way to the car said, "Mary, you'll have things running like a fine-oiled machine in no time at all." She was known for her housekeeping skills, her excellent cooking, and her talent for organization. All would be handled efficiently during the next few weeks, he knew.

Bonnie sat in the back seat, the little pink dog in her lap. Mark drove extra carefully on that pre-seatbelt afternoon, sensing precious cargo behind him. Within minutes they arrived at the home Mary and Mark had built only two years before. It was the second house they had built and the third they had lived in since their marriage.

The last one, a four-bedroom two-story brick structure, had waited to be filled by children who never came. This home, downsized to two bedrooms, was designed for the childless couple that they were. There was a large living room, a dining room for entertaining, and a two-car garage in a neighborhood of one-car garages. It was only a block from the country club where Mary golfed and played bridge while Mark struggled to find time to utilize his membership.

Mary and Mark slept in separate bedrooms. His snoring was loud and unrelenting. Mary had twin beds in her room, and Mark's room had a double bed. For the duration of the visit, Bonnie would sleep in the other twin bed in Mary's room. It was where they led her when they first entered the house. Her little suitcase was brought into the room, and the items filled one drawer in the dresser.

Mary let Bonnie help with that task, then it was time for a nap. Bonnie figured out quickly enough that she was to rest in that pretty bed with the violets on the bedspread. The drapes were closed against the afternoon sunlight, and soon she was in dreamland. But, dreams led to nightmares and bedwetting, and the couple rushed in to find a sobbing child too traumatized to speak. It was the beginning of many nights of screams and soaked sheets. If Mary tired of this bedwetting routine, she never said, but certain modifications were made to help with the problem.

Drinking water was eliminated earlier in the evening and plastic mattress covers were purchased. Many nightgowns were eventually bought, so changing from one to the other was quick. But at the moment, on this first afternoon, they were just as frightened as the child. They wondered what could possibly cause this type of behavior. It certainly seemed true, as Dorothy had said, that Bonnie had not adjusted to life in America.

Tears dried and clothes changed, Bonnie looked at Mary and said in German, "Are you my new mommy?" Mary was shocked. Why would she say that? Did Dorothy tell her to?

"No, Honey, you can call us Aunt Mary and Uncle Mark." Her German must have been adequate enough to convey the message. Soon *Tante* Mary served dinner and noticed that Bonnie was eating like she had never seen food in her life, chattering away about anything and everything while "aunt and uncle" sat and listened, unable to interpret all that she said. They smiled and laughed, enjoying the little German girl's visit.

Despite a nap, Bonnie was exhausted when bedtime came. Mary worried about whether Bonnie would have another nightmare. She hoped it was a one-time thing, brought on by the train ride, the separation from her mother, and the surroundings of a new environment. Unfortunately, the nightmare returned often – and for many years. And never, ever, would Bonnie describe it.

I knew exactly what the nightmare was, but I could not articulate it at that time. Later, when I spoke English well, I would never reveal what it was to my parents. It was too terrifying to speak out loud. Until the writing of this book, I had never told anyone. You can be the judge of how awful this nightmare would be for a four-year-old.

I remember the nightmare clearly, although I never told Mary and Mark the details no matter how many times they asked. In actuality, I felt I could never say the words out loud. Speaking of the nightmare seemed even more frightening than actually having it. It couldn't have been real. But, where does a four-year-old come up with such a dream?

I wake in the darkness of a very small upstairs room with a slanted roof. There is a window at the foot of my single bed, and through the sheer curtains I can see that it is night. I hear laughter. People are downstairs talking loudly. I slip through the door. In only my nightgown, I slowly descend steep steps. I walk into a bright room full of men and women. They are lifting glasses of amber to their lips. They are having fun.

For some reason I continue to walk to the center of the room. No one seems to notice or care that I am there and out of bed, not sleeping. On the davenport a lady sits, and I stand directly in front of her. Someone staggers drunkenly into the back of the davenport and the lady's head falls forward and onto the floor. I don't remember how anyone else at the party reacted, but I screamed, and that is the point where I would always wake up needing to be changed because I had wet the bed.

Did I have the nightmare before I arrived in La Crosse? I don't know. I had it for many years after until finally the horror of it slid away.

Chapter Ten

A Year in Limbo

And so, my life in Wisconsin began. Often, Aunt Mary had little tasks for me to perform. One of my first was to sit properly at the kitchen table. It was covered with a plastic cloth so I could draw on coloring books with crayons. I hadn't seen coloring books before and had to be shown how to use the crayons. As I began my project, Aunt Mary removed the crayon from my left hand and placed it in my right. I would use my right hand until I picked up a new color and then I continued with my left hand until she noticed and made me change again.

There were daily lessons in English. Mary couldn't believe that Dorothy had not taught me any English. "What is this?"

"*Apfel.*"

"No, apple. Say it again."

"What is this?"

"*Fleisch?*"

"No, meat. Repeat it, please."

Eventually, the grocery store game became less stressful as answers were given correctly. Mary overheard me telling my doll, "In America you have to eat things even if you don't like them." Nouns were easier for me, but I mostly spoke my sentences half in German and half in

English ("*Das ist die watermelon nicht der apple*") which didn't seem to bother my sandbox playmates. Mary and Mark, however, were worried about the stigma of a German accent. They worked very hard to eliminate my "Germanness."

We went on educational trips to the store. As we walked around, Mary would tell me the name of an item in English and I was to repeat it. At home I had to arrange items in categories of fruits vs. vegetables, or by color, and eventually I did learn.

Mary cooked three meals a day. For breakfast we had either oatmeal, eggs and bacon, or pancakes. I loved the pancakes. Oatmeal made me gag, but I learned quickly that I had to eat what was put in front of me. I wouldn't have argued anyway, but it was evident I had no choice and I ate what I was told to eat.

Lunch was usually soup and a sandwich or fruit salad with a homemade muffin. Leftovers were creative. Mary was a wonderful cook and I think I liked most everything. What I didn't like—liver, lamb shanks, sardines— were served with mashed potatoes, corn, or Jell-O with fruit to make my dislikes more tolerable.

Aunt Mary also loved to bake, so the counters were often adorned with pies, caramel rolls, or cakes. We didn't snack between meals so none of us gained weight, although Uncle Mark was caught from time-to-time sneaking ice cream. I wasn't privy to conversations about this transgression.

I was content. I guess I forgot Dorothy, although I was told that she would be coming back for me "in a couple weeks." When you're four, how do you know about the passage of time? I loved going to park during the day to swing, watch the monkeys, or ride the little kid-sized boats. I was unaware that my caretakers were waiting for an air-mail letter from Germany. My too-few clothes were increased when Aunt Mary took me downtown to the local department store for dresses, shoes, and play clothes.

I was not allowed to have anything to drink after supper because of my bedwetting. I would try to sneakily suck water off the toothbrush, but Mary noticed and watched me more closely. I remember being very thirsty at night. I guess I didn't get the correlation between water in, water out.

Mary and Mark received the first letter from my mother three weeks after I arrived—already later than they expected. The postmark was from Germany. When they opened the letter, it confirmed that Dorothy was not back in the United States. On the contrary, she would be delayed a few more weeks and could she impose on them to keep me a little longer? Mary wrote immediately. "Of course we'd be happy to keep her for another couple weeks." Uncle Mark drove two miles to the post office for the late afternoon pickup. I'm told that explanations to me about my mother's whereabouts were met with some indifference on my part.

I suppose she was out of sight and therefore out of mind. My reality was playing with my dolls and making neighborhood friends and a 45 record player that continuously spun with my new Disney records. Also, I was taken wherever Mary and Mark went. If they went out to eat, I went also. If they went to friend's houses for cards, I was there sleeping in the guest bedroom. I met some of the grandchildren of these friends and I continued to learn English. I enjoyed swinging, swimming, and playing with the collie next door. It kept my days filled and my mind occupied.

I'm sure Mary worried that I would miss Dorothy, and I probably did, but without the ability to express the words in English, or in German for that matter, I said nothing. Mary considered it odd that I didn't ask about her. Mark said to leave well enough alone.

Dorothy's original request for a month turned into two before another letter arrived. She was still not in the United States. She was busy in Germany, working hard to eliminate tuberculosis, a disease that ran rampant in Europe during the war. The letter asked only for an extension of another month. "Well, in for a penny, in for pound," was Mark's response. "Truth be told," he said, "I like having Bonnie around." They both worried in private about becoming too attached to me, but for the moment there was no other choice.

Mary wrote to Dorothy in late summer, "When are you returning for Bonnie? Can we put her in nursery school? It would help with her socialization skills and her English. She needs friends to play with." The answer came quickly, "Yes, certainly." As Christmas approached, Mary wrote to Dorothy again. "Will you be back by Christmas? If not, we will buy Bonnie some gifts and some new clothes, as she is growing."

A letter came.

"I can't be home by Christmas. Please, keep her for the holidays. And give her this handkerchief. Tell her it's from her Mommy."

I'm sure I loved that Christmas. There are photos to support my memories, or at least they ensure that I have them. A big, beautiful tree and me in a new pink robe and fluffy slippers with a grin from ear to ear. There was a tin dollhouse under the tree and a tricycle next to it; a doll and a doll bed with a side rail that pushed up and down. Was it overwhelming to receive so many presents and partake in such a lavish Christmas holiday? I don't know, I wasn't aware of it.

There was extended family visiting on Christmas Eve and Mary served the traditional oyster stew. I didn't like it. Aunt Mary allowed me to eat the oyster crackers only after I was assured they were not made out of oysters. *How in the world did I even know what an oyster was?* Christmas Eve was supposed to be about fasting and preparing for the birth of Christ, although we did open some gifts that night.

After the Christmas Eve meal was finished and the dishes were cleared from the table and washed (by hand, of course—there was no electric dishwasher in this household) we then could all go into the formal living room and Uncle Mark would start the wood fire in the fireplace. It could not be burning at any time if no one was in the room because it might cause a house fire. The entire time, as we opened presents, Uncle Mark sat on an ottoman very close to the fireplace. Later, when I was older, I found out he was deathly afraid of fire and his fear was exacerbated by the fact that a dead, dry tree was only a few feet from his greatest fear—errant flames.

In hindsight, I know without a doubt that he was poised to extinguish any possible fire, or die trying, to save the people he loved. Christmas Day was attending Mass, where we celebrated His birth and later a lavish noontime feast at our house with family and friends. Food and gifts from Santa were in abundance.

January loomed, cold and white. The Spettels normally took a vacation to Florida. Another letter flew to Germany. Could they be allowed to take me to Florida with them? Dorothy's answer, "Yes, but I will be home soon." I didn't have a clue what *Florida* was, but Aunt Mary seemed very excited about it and she said it was a long drive. *I wonder if I equated it with crossing an ocean.* It took several days in the car to get to this warm, sunny place. At 4 o'clock each afternoon, on the drive down, we started the search for motel vacancy signs along the way. After we checked in I was allowed to swim in the small outdoor pool that was always there. I liked swimming and, of course, swimming was safe because Uncle Mark never let me out of his sight when I was near the water.

I clearly remember as we drove deeper into the south, stopping at a place called a cafeteria, and Aunt Mary explained that we would go through a line and get to take whatever food we thought looked good. She also told me that there would be people behind the cafeteria line who had dark skin. They were called Negroes and I was not to comment on the color of their skin. I was fearful and kept my eyes downcast during my first encounter with a person of color.

Mary had a reservation at our final destination, but the room was not cleaned yet. Anxious to introduce me to the ocean, Aunt Mary told me to change into my swimsuit in the back seat of the car. I remember looking out of the tiny windows in the back, worried that someone might look in. I loved my suit, which was new for the trip; it was a cute leopard print.

After being lathered with Coppertone, a smell that will forever remind me of beaches and sand and donning white-framed sunglasses, I took Uncle Mark's extended hand and curiously walked to the edge of the water. We waded in up to our knees and finally got all wet. It was fun and different from the above ground pool at the La Crosse Country Club where I had to climb a ladder and then jump in. The waves washed around my legs and the sand was warm. Building sandcastles was wonderful with Uncle Mark helping me.

Mary and Mark continued their faux parenthood. They tried not to become too attached, but it must have been difficult to have someone live in their house—someone who depended on them for everything—and not be attached. Meantime, I was oblivious to any tension on their part. I liked school, I had friends in the neighborhood, I was starting to communicate well, and I was thriving on Aunt Mary's good cooking. I was busy with my toy horses, my roller skates, my bubble-blowing kit, hopscotch, and my dolls. If I thought of my mother, I don't remember.

Letters continued to cross the ocean in both directions. *Dorothy was busy with her work. She missed me. She would be home soon. She could not come home just yet. She wanted to see me.* Mark and Mary had deep discussions late into the night. During the months I had been there, they had come to love me.

How could they give me up after all this time? They sent a letter to Germany in the spring of 1953 and asked Dorothy if she might consider letting them adopt me. They anxiously awaited the answer. When it came, it was postmarked Wilmington, Delaware. "No, Bonnie is MY daughter. Please bring her back now."

Mary and Mark's hearts were heavy. Mary had tears in her eyes when she read the letter.   "What more can we do?" Mary lamented.

Mark replied, "That's the way it is. It's always been in God's hands." The little German girl whom they had met on the ship almost a year earlier had been with them for many months, but the end was near. Those original few weeks for my visit had turned into almost a year. So much change, so much learning, so much growth for me. So much happiness, so much fun, so much distraction for them.

In a week, Mary was packing a new, bigger suitcase with clothes and toys. She told me we were going to ride the train all the way to Delaware and I was going to join my mother.

I don't remember that her statement meant anything to me. I'm sure I might have been excited about going on a trip, but the reason would not have been revealed to me by Mary or Mark. Did I notice they were sad? Extra clingy? No, I was a child. And now I wonder what my folks thought about having to be the ones to make the trip out East, instead of Dorothy coming for me herself.

Me, four years old, in my leopard swimsuit in Florida.

Chapter Eleven

June 1953—The Train Ride

And so the day of the trip began. Tears were concealed while Mary and Mark closed the suitcases for this sad trip. Stoic Mary would never show her anguish at having to give me up. Possibly she would indulge her heartbreak on the way home.

We were driven to the Burlington train station by Betty and Frank Hoeschler. Frank was initially married to Mark's aunt, and after she passed away he married Mary's sister. The few times that Mary had to be gone from the house during the day for something, I was dropped off at the Hoeschler mansion. And it *was* a mansion, with a grand staircase. Think *Gone with the Wind.*

On the train we found our sleeper car. Uncle Mark slept on the top bunk and Aunt Mary and I slept together on the bottom one. The first night, she had me sleep on the inside so I wouldn't fall out. *It is my first conscious memory of being claustrophobic.* It was horrible. I couldn't move because of the wall on one side of me and a person on the other. I didn't want to wake her up, so I lay in one spot, twitching but silent, waiting until sleep finally overcame me, only to wake and experience the feeling again. *To this day, I can't even stand to be the inside person at a booth in a restaurant.*

During the daytime we sat in the dome car. It was so exciting to have a 360-degree-view as we clicked along the tracks. I found if I looked out to the side it made me feel nauseous, but staring straight ahead was fine. We would eat in the dining car. A Negro man in a crisp white uniform showed us to the table and fussed over me. I thought he was delightful. He made a big show of presenting my children's menu and snapping out my napkin. There was not much for a five-year-old to do on a train. The second afternoon I lost a tooth and Mary put it in a napkin on the sink.

She told me that the Tooth Fairy would come in the night and give me a dime. I had no idea what a dime was, but it sounded good to me. Unfortunately, the porter for our room came in to clean up and get the beds ready for sleeping, and he threw the tooth away. Mary was more devastated than I was. I can still remember that. She believed that the Tooth Fairy would only leave a dime if he or she got the tooth in exchange. I remember wondering what they did with it, and also being afraid of this stranger who was coming into my room when I slept.

We arrived in Delaware. At our hotel, Mark called Dorothy from the room. They arranged for her to meet us at the hotel for the transfer (of me) and have one last lunch—the four of us. Lunchtime came too soon for the grieving couple. This would be their last few hours with me. *I didn't know it was supposed to be my last few hours with them.*

We waited outside the entrance to the hotel dining room and Dorothy came toward us. Mary expected me to run to her, but I acted like I didn't even know who she was. Dorothy immediately became angry with the Spettels, accusing them of trying to make me forget her. Mary denied any such thing. In fact, Mary said, she had talked of Dorothy often, but had only one picture of her to show me: one Mary had taken on the *SS United States*. Dorothy calmed down and they entered the dining room.

It was a large, elegant restaurant with many waiters bustling to serve diners. At noon the tables were dressed more casually than in the evening when they were set with linen and sterling. For lunch, it was placemats and less ostentatious utensils, and the water was served in plain goblets instead of the crystal reserved for the later hours. We were seated and food was ordered. *I'm not sure what I ate, and I wonder who got the privilege of ordering for me—Mary or Dorothy.*

Mary and Mark wanted to ask questions of Dorothy. Where in the world had she been all this time? What had kept her from her daughter for almost a year? Why did she think she could dump a child on nearly complete strangers and just assume that it would be okay? None of those words were spoken. In 1953 those kinds of things were not asked and polite conversation ensued instead. *How are you? Hot weather we're having. Is your chicken good?*

I'm sure I felt the undertones of discomfort among the three of them. There must have been some tension. Two women were struggling to keep their tempers in rein while one man hoped to avoid a blowup. Finally, the meal cleared. Mark broached, one more time, the possibility of Dorothy letting them adopt me. His arguments were: You have your career; you have ties to Germany; you are so busy; you didn't reunite with your family; you have no husband or other help caring for Bonnie. This was followed by: We have money; we have grown to love Bonnie; we are so happy to have her in our lives; we'd be so good to her; she would thrive on the advantages we could offer.

Dorothy was flummoxed. She seemed to sway. Dorothy wasn't sure. She loved me. She couldn't live without me. "But you did," countered Mary. "You lived without her for a year." Finally, somewhere in the conversation about my future, Dorothy agreed that they would make better parents by virtue of the fact that, if nothing else, there were two of them.

Mark grabbed the waiter, borrowed a pen, and wrote out a "declaration of intent to adopt" on the white paper placemat. He asked her to sign and date it. She did. Then he asked her to shake on it. She did. The older couple was overjoyed. Their dream had come true. I would be theirs. The trip of despair had turned around to one of joy.

However, it was late on Friday. Some legal arrangements would need to be made. Some papers created and signed. Dorothy offered to send the papers to them in La Crosse, but Mary said she would prefer to have the papers in place before they left for home. The three of them agreed to meet on Tuesday to see a lawyer, as Monday was a holiday.

Mary said they would love to go to New York City to introduce me to her nephew and his wife. We would make a little trip over the weekend and call Dorothy on Tuesday morning. They said they would stay at the Commodore Hotel. They hopped on the train Friday evening and went immediately to the hotel. As they entered, they discovered that there was construction in the lobby. Mary immediately canceled the reservation and we grabbed a taxi and went to The St. Moritz.

We had a grand time in New York, I've been told. We went to the Bronx Zoo and I enjoyed seeing the great variety of animals not present in our little zoo back in La Crosse. I even got to feed the elephants, standing on the fence with Uncle Mark holding me tight so I didn't fall. It was the first time I remember someone being frightened for me. It was palpable through Mark's fingertips. He cared so much and loved me so much and feared so much for my safety. *That would never change, ever.*

After a fun weekend, we took the train back to Delaware on Monday night and checked into the same hotel we had stayed at before. Mary called Dorothy immediately and was greeted with fury. Where had they been? She had tried to call them at the hotel they said they would be at and they were not there. She thought they had stolen her daughter. Mary explained about the construction. Her heart was doing flip-flops because Dorothy's tone was angry and unforgiving. Mary's instincts were correct: Dorothy had changed her mind.

Of course, I didn't know how crestfallen Uncle Mark and Aunt Mary probably were. I'm sure I was exhausted from the New York adventure, sound asleep in my bed. I imagine that they agonized over Dorothy's reversal for a long time that night.

Chapter Twelve

A Change of Heart

Dorothy was still furious when they met the next afternoon. She said she had consulted with a friend of hers and had decided that she wanted to keep me. Mary and Mark asked, suspiciously, if they could meet this friend. Mary asked to speak with him in private while Mark and Dorothy and I sat on the large sofa in the lobby. Mary told the male friend that she was concerned that Dorothy might not be a very stable influence on me. She seemed to be having trouble settling into a place, seemed to be having trouble giving up her life in Germany, and seemed to have very wide mood swings.

The man was the head librarian at a library in Wilmington and Dorothy's friend, but he quietly told Mary, "Do everything you can to keep Bonnie; Dorothy is not capable of taking care of her right now. Be firm with her." After a hasty goodbye to Dorothy he left, and Dorothy, Mark, Mary and I stood in the lobby. Mark asked her for a little more time with me—just until after supper—and it was agreed she would return for me later. But she would not be giving me up or falling for any tricks, she admonished.

As soon as Dorothy was out of sight, Mary told her husband what Dorothy's companion had said. Mark said he was thinking that she seemed unstable to him, too. They jumped into a taxi and went to the superior court in Wilmington. Once there, Mark found a judge (the Honorable Caleb R. Layton III) who would give them a few minutes of his time. Mark went into a big room while Mary and I sat on a long, wooden bench along the wall in a hallway with very tall ceilings. *I stared at the ceiling, the tiled floor, and the industrial paint on the walls, probably wondering what kind of hotel this was; certainly not as pretty as the St. Moritz in New York.*

In a little while Mark came out and sat with me while Mary went in to talk to the judge. Then it was my turn to go into the big room beyond the oak doors. A woman greeted me and told me her name and said she would be with me while I was in that room. I only had to answer some questions and I'd see my aunt and uncle very soon. A man sat at a large table and he asked me questions, most of them I probably didn't understand, but I imagine I told him what I could. I loved Aunt Mary and Uncle Mark, I had fun with them, I loved school and life in my neighborhood and I didn't know who Dorothy was. She was kind of scary because she kept shouting and then she'd hug me and then she'd cry and then she'd laugh and then she'd shout again.

Mark told me later that the judge had said, "This Dorothy sounds like a nut case. Take Bonnie and just go back to La Crosse." Mark told the judge, "No, we'd be looking over our shoulders for the rest of our lives and I won't live that way."

Later that afternoon, Mary called Dorothy. "Come get Bonnie." Dorothy asked if they wanted to have a last meal together and Mary said she didn't. Their hearts were breaking and they just wanted to get it over with, get back to La Crosse and resume their lives and forget the past year.

Mark couldn't go to the lobby and watch while Dorothy took possession of me. He stayed in the hotel room and cried. Mary, stronger than Mark in every way, took me down in the elevator to the lobby. Dorothy was waiting. We walked up to her, my baby doll in my arms, my new suitcase held by Mary. Dorothy seemed subdued. She looked at Mary and said, "I know you probably would be wonderful parents. I don't have the means to care for a child now, but I don't know how I could give her up and never see her. If I let you adopt her, would you let me see her from time to time? Be part of her life?"

Mary's answer was firm. "No. If we adopt her, we are her parents, and I don't want to have an arrangement like that." Mary hugged and kissed me, turned on her heel and disappeared into the elevator.

As she put the key in the hotel room door, Mary heard the phone ring through her sobs. Mark answered. He listened for several minutes. Suddenly his face changed from pain to joy. "We'll be right down." He hung up the phone. Mary looked at him, a tiny seed of hope finding its way into her heavy chest. "What?"

Mark jumped up from the bed, pulling on his suit pants, coat, and shoes. "Hurry, she's changed her mind. She said we should have Bonnie. She'll be better off with us. Hurry! Hurry!" They ran for the elevator. It was delayed many floors above them. They turned to the stairs and ran down two flights to the lobby. There, Dorothy and I sat. The minute I saw them, I ran to them for a hug.

I'm sure my brain had not comprehended why I had been left in the lobby with this strange lady and now I understood. It was only to be for a few minutes. That was okay. I was afraid they were not coming back, but I knew that couldn't be the case.

Mark shook Dorothy's hand, Mary hugged her. Mark hurried back up to the room to retrieve a prepared adoption document drawn up before our trip by Judge Leonard Roraff for just such a possibility. Dorothy signed it. Mark told Dorothy they would be going back to La Crosse the next day. He needed to get back to work. Mostly he wanted to put some distance between Dorothy and me. Mary was still stunned. Dorothy said that she would have the judge's office send over the consent papers in the morning.

We took the train back to Wisconsin the next day after the papers arrived. The scenery was the same, only in reverse. I thought I'd had a grand adventure and was unaware of the momentous life-changing events that led to me riding back on this train, back to La Crosse, back to my house, and my school, and my friends, back to my books, and the baby bed that my doll slept in, back to my tricycle and the swing set put up in early spring because I loved to swing so much, back to normal, back to a two-parent household and safety and security and schedules, rules and consequences.

Mark had to return to Delaware once to get more paperwork signed. Judge Roraff strongly suggested that they break all ties with Dorothy after hearing about all the strange circumstances since she had left me the summer before. It was surmised that Dorothy returned to Europe shortly after and ended up back with her ex-husband (they had divorced in 1940). In later correspondence, her last name had changed.

That night, after a long train ride from Delaware back to La Crosse, at midnight, before either of them went to bed, Mary and Mark both sat down and wrote about the circumstances that had occurred from the time they left on the train until they returned to the house on Hackberry Lane. Mark wrote by hand—I still have it—on a piece of typing paper. Mary typed a letter to her sister in California. At the end of the letter *(I have a carbon copy of it)* she said that that day, the day we returned to La Crosse, was a year to the day since they had said goodbye to me on the *SS United States*.

And I slept soundly. There were no nightmares to disturb my sleep that night, just contentment that I was back in my bed, back to my own house, back to my new reality.

Chapter Thirteen

Child of The Heart

When I returned to Wisconsin with Mary and Mark I had no idea that anything was different. I didn't know that they had not expected me to return with them. I didn't know that I had been given up twice—once by my birth mother and then, only a few days earlier, by my second mother, Dorothy. Mary and Mark were ecstatic. Mary immediately quit working with Mark at their store. She had a new full-time job, and she took it seriously.

There were more English lessons. I was getting better but still interspersed German words in my sentences. *"Ist das on the inside utter die outside?"* *"Macht the licht out."* *"Wo ist my friend?"* Mary was patient. She had a young child to mold into a perfect little American girl who would hopefully morph into a perfect young lady who would slip into the role of a perfect wife and mother. *I don't think that I ever accomplished any of those "perfect roles," but I do know I tried my darndest.*

Mary and Mark were Catholic. I had been baptized Catholic by Dorothy on September 1, 1948, so we know I was living with her barely a month after I was born. No information has ever been found to enlighten us on when my transfer to her took place, probably immediately after my birth. No matter, it did happen and now, in September of 1953, I was ready to start kindergarten. Mary had previously asked Dorothy if I had any siblings that Mary and Mark might adopt and raise along with me, but she told them there were not. I was destined to be an only child.

In retrospect, I am sure the Spettels were of an age where a traditional adoption would not have been approved. I remember one day Mary telling me that a lady was coming to talk to me and I was to be polite and tell her that I liked my new home and loved my new parents.

I remember that lady coming to the door. I remember Mary being very nervous. I must have said the right things and Mary must have cleaned the house well enough because no one took me away. Now I know the lady must have been with social services, or what passed for social services back in the early '50s. On November 9, 1953, I was taken in front of Judge Lincoln Neprud in La Crosse to have my life forever entwined with Mary and Mark's. I was to become a Spettel with all it entailed. I would, for the second time, become a "child of the heart." This time I would grow in Mary and Mark's hearts.

My new parents were well off. I didn't realize that then, of course. They were older, established, and that meant that they could take me on trips, afford to buy nice toys and clothes for me, and later send me to private schools. Mother had dreams of me attending Vassar or Radcliff. *Poor Mary, how different reality was from her expectations; the expectations I never lived up to.*

I can't remember much about kindergarten except sitting at a little wooden chair in a half circle in the front of the room while the teacher taught our small group. Each reading group had a name and it denoted how smart you were. *I wonder if I was a guppy, a whale, or a walrus.* I probably didn't come across as very smart considering I was still transitioning from German to English.

I do remember I pulled the chair out from under the little girl who was in front of me after we said the Pledge of Allegiance, and she fell to the floor. Go figure: Sixty-some years later, we are still friends.

In first grade my mother enrolled me at Blessed Sacrament School, the Catholic grade school attached to our church. After the first day, she removed me and put me in Emerson Elementary, a public school near our home. She was angry that the class sizes were too large at the Catholic school and felt I would not get enough attention. The law said the public schools had to control their class sizes. By second grade, the church council had approved hiring another teacher and I went back to second grade at Blessed Sacrament with Sister Louise Regine as my teacher.

To this day her name stirs feelings of fear. Even my mother, years later, admitted being afraid of her. I'm sure she was probably one of those nuns who was forced to become a teacher rather than follow a path more suited to her.

I was never an outstanding student. My report cards were interspersed with G's for "good work" and I's for "needs improvement." Back in those days, teachers wrote comments on our report cards and mine always said things like, "Needs to pay attention," or "Converses too much with her neighbors." It also indicated what I liked— art. I loved to draw and, in later years, I got compliments on my creative writing skills. I didn't like arithmetic, but Mark worked with me. It eventually got easier...until freshman year when I took Algebra. *Who in the world invented Algebra?*

Life was normal. I was good, I was bad, I tested my parents, I acquiesced to my parents, but I did what most girls did back then: obeyed, honored, accepted.

Me mixing mud pies
in our back yard.

My mother loved
'posed' pictures and
she kept ALL of them.

Chapter Fourteen

1956—Naturalization

On November 8, 1956, I became an American citizen. The cost was $10.00. Up until that day my mother planned for my middle name to be Jean (it was on my adoption papers) after the young woman who had died of leukemia right before their trip to Europe—that fateful trip when they met me. Mary Jean Spettel was listed on my official petition for naturalization, but on the *day* of the ceremony, Mother decided to change it to Susan. I can vividly remember her bending down and telling me my name would not be Mary Jean anymore; I would be Mary Susan and I had to write that on the forms I would be signing in a few minutes.

I remember being nervous. How did I spell Susan? She said she would explain when we got home, but I don't remember an explanation that day or anytime. I do know I felt confused. I was petrified that I would do something wrong, that the judge would ask me a question I could not answer, or that I would forget how to say the Pledge of Allegiance, which I had practiced over and over. I don't think I had a clue what was really happening—that I was becoming an American citizen. *I already lived in America; what was going to be different?*

I went back to school that afternoon. The teacher called me to her desk and handed me a storybook, asking me to go to the first-grade classroom to read to them. *Me! I was so proud.* Other kids in my classroom had been given this honor in the past, but I was never one to distinguish myself and so I was completely taken by surprise. I thought that my teacher must think a lot of me. In 15 minutes, I had completed my task and returned to my homeroom where my teacher stood behind our large round reading table with my mother at her side. As I entered all the children shouted "Congratulations!" and applauded.

My mother had planned a little party to celebrate my naturalization. The kids had cards for me and seemed very excited about what I had just gone through. *What? Didn't everyone go through such a ceremony?* Mother had brought cake and juice for my classmates. It was she who had worked it out with Sister to have me leave the room while they set the party up. Later that night as I was falling asleep, I remember the disappointment I felt as I realized that my "so-called honor" to read to the first graders was just a ruse to get me out of the room.

It's interesting, in retrospect, that I don't remember ever being teased because I was foreign-born, or because I just recently became an American citizen, or that my English wasn't perfect. It might have been a bonus for me that there was an Asian boy in my class. He was also adopted. Despite our common path, we never became friends. He was very shy—I wasn't. I was a flighty, social butterfly.

My naturalization in 1956. I'm on the bottom right, holding the flag.

Chapter Fifteen

What's in a Name?

I have had so many names. I was born Gerda Erika Paul. I was confirmed Mary Christiane Suzan Elliot. In 1953 I was adopted as Mary Jean Spettel and naturalized as Mary Susan Spettel. I can throw in my confirmation name of Bernadette, just in case you want to know that. When I married I became Mary Susan Willemssen. As you might have noticed, no mention of Bonnie so far, however all throughout my life I was called Bonnie. Teachers called me Mary; friends from school would call me Mary, neighbors, relatives, and anyone I met outside of school called me Bonnie.

My second adoptive mother's name was Mary, also. It was often confusing in our household when someone would call on the phone. My dad would always respond, when he answered the phone, "Do you want big Mary or little Mary?" I never introduced myself as Mary, but I always had to write it for any official documents. I had to sign checks with Mary as my name. I had to take out a loan, order something from a catalogue, all with that name on my official documents. Many times I'd ignore someone calling "Mary" across a parking lot, not realizing they were speaking to me

My *Geburtsurkunde* (birth certificate), at least the one that my first adoptive mother gave to my second adoptive mother, said I was born on

30 July, 1948 in Lichtenberg. This area of Berlin, Germany later was part of the Eastern sector when Berlin was divided. It said my *Vater* (father) was a *Kraftwagenfuhrer* (taxi driver) named Gerhard Benno Hermann Paul. My mother was Erika Gerda Irene Paul (maiden name: Müller).

In the first years in America, I had only a tiny 3" x 4" piece of paper stating when I was born and where. It was issued by the Department of Immigration and Naturalization, but printed on it were the words *not proof of citizenship.*

September 1, 1948: I was baptized according to the rite of the Roman Catholic Church in McNair Barracks Chapel in Berlin, Germany. Dorothy, my second mother, was in the U.S. Army.

February 1950: a copy of my birth certificate saying I was born on July 30, 1948, is in my file of papers. However, there is no explanation for why it has the date 1950 on it, but it is the most official paper I had until my brother Dieter found another one that went back even farther.

June 1952: The office of the Council General of the United States of America, City of Frankfurt-an-Main, Germany sent a letter certifying the adoption decree of Gerda Erika Paul was true and accurate. It was signed by Wayne W. Fisher, vice-council.

July 1952: I was admitted to the United States as a quota immigrant for permanent residence.

I had a passport when Mary and Mark adopted me—with Dorothy's last name after my own. It had numerous stamps on it showing trips to France and Switzerland. I know now, after locating the nanny who traveled with us, that we accompanied Dorothy on her business trips. The picture on the passport is one of only six pictures I had of myself before the age of four until 2018, when Dorothy's granddaughter, thankfully, sent me a few more.

July 1953: Dorothy signed papers giving consent for Mary and Mark to adopt me. The reasons she gave were "unexpected and unpredictable difficulties, of financial and other nature, in the best interests of the child." Dorothy had sent papers ascertaining that she was my adoptive mother, having given me the name Mary Christianne Susanne Elliot.

July 1953. The U.S. Dept. of Justice Immigration and Naturalization Service in Rochester, Minnesota, returned my German passport to the attorney (and later judge) Leonard Roraff—a good friend of Mary and Mark. My adopted mother, Mary, kept everything, for which I am grateful. I know that a man named Hans P. Hansen, Investigator, wrote a letter to Judge Roraff that I was eligible, according to the Immigration and Nationality Act of 1952, to become a citizen if I lived in the U.S. for two years and had one year's physical presence in the house of the adopted parents. The letter was in response to Mary and Mark's inquiry on procedures to adopt me.

July 30 1953: When I was five years old the law firm that Mark and Mary hired to clear the way for my adoption wrote and said that I was eligible for naturalization at the proper time.

September 2, 1953: Dorothy had to appear before a Notary Public and state that she was my legal parent having been given that right by a "duly constituted court having jurisdiction in the city of Frankfurt-on-Main, Germany." It went on to show exhibits A and B which gave my birth name as Gerda Erika Paul. It also stated that Dorothy was unmarried at the time of that rendering, that she had been divorced in 1940, and that her former husband had no legal rights in this adoption matter.

November 1953: La Crosse County. My adoption was official. I was named Mary Jean Spettel.

March 1956: A letter arrived from the Catholic Welfare Guild. Mary had written requesting a copy of my Baptismal Certificate. The Guild tried to contact Dorothy and found that she had moved to a different house. They spoke with her and she said that she did not have a copy of the certificate, but was sure that it could be obtained through the Military Ordinariate or the War Relief Services/National Catholic Welfare Conference—both in New York City.

March 1956: Mark and Mary got a copy of my official baptism papers from the Military Ordinariate in New York City.

June 1956: Mary and Mark file a petition for naturalization on my behalf. They had to meet an examiner at the Office of Clerk of Circuit

Court and bring two witnesses who had known them for more than five years. *I don't know this for a fact, but I'm sure they brought along Betty and Frank Hoeschler, my godparents in La Crosse.*

October 1956: A letter came, addressed to me—Mary Jean Spettel— to present myself on November 8, 1956, and bring my alien registration receipt card. It would be the final hearing on my petition for naturalization.

November 8, 1956: The day I became a naturalized citizen of the United States of America and became Mary Susan Spettel.

June 1962: Mary, Mark, and I traveled to Germany, Austria, and France. I was on the *same* passport as my mother and there was no notification on it of where I was born. That was a good thing because when we were in West Berlin, we were allowed to take a daytime bus tour into East Berlin as *Americans*; I would not have been allowed, as a former German national, to enter the Russian sector of Berlin. My poor dad died a thousand deaths worrying about my *birthplace* becoming known. He warned me not to mention it to anyone at all from the moment we entered Germany until we left. He forbade me to speak to the Russian officers when they boarded the bus to check passports and IDs and, if asked, I was to lie and say I was born in La Crosse, Wisconsin. This was the first and only time my father ever advocated lying. I'm sure he confessed it in the confessional when he got home.

June 1966: Mary requested a birth certificate from the Immigration Department in Milwaukee, Wisconsin. She explained I needed it for a planned trip to Mexico, and the travel agency had said it was necessary to get a 'travel card" for me.

June 1966: Mary wrote to the State Board of Health, Bureau of Vital Statistics, in Madison, Wisconsin stating that she felt that the birth certificate I currently possessed gave too much information on me. She asked if it would be possible to get a birth certificate that simply stated my birth and country "that would be adequate for her future use whenever a birth certificate was necessary."

July 1966: The Wisconsin State Board of Health wrote a letter saying they would send the birth form (G-350) as soon as possible.

July 1966: Mary wrote to the Immigration and Naturalization Services in Chicago, Illinois and said that she had been advised by Madison, Wisconsin to send a certified copy of the Order of Adoption and that they would issue a Certification of Birth data form in the adoptive name. "This form (G-350) sets forth the name and sex of the child and the date and place of birth." In the letter my folks stated they wanted to keep my name as close as possible to my original baptismal name of Mary Christianne Susanne and that is why they changed my name from Mary Jean Spettel (on my adoption papers) to Mary Susan (on my naturalization papers).

September 1966: Mary received a copy of a G-350 form, issued on my behalf. It was in preparation for going to Mexico on vacation. Until this time I did not have a U.S. passport or a U.S. birth certificate, and oddly, now that I think back, I didn't even realize it. Now I had an official piece of paper called a Certification of Birth Data issued by the Department of Justice with the name Mary Susan Spettel.

On April 29, 1972, I married Jim and became Mary Susan Willemssen. I never really liked my last name—Spettel. It was hard to pronounce and I did not like that when I wrote in cursive, two letters of my name went below the line—the "y" and the "p." I was still called Bonnie by everyone who knew me well, but in the grocery store, the clerk would call me *Mary* after she looked at my check. I would look around to see who she was talking to. In the bank, they would address me as *Mary*, and I'd wonder where *she* (my mother) was.

March 1977: Mary and Mark tried to contact my second mother, Dorothy. They didn't know if she was still alive, but they hoped that she or her son would be able to give them some medical information on my birth family. Jim and I had a baby who died in February of 1977 of birth defects and we wondered if it might have been a genetic disorder.

April 1986: Mary and Mark contacted Jerome, Dorothy's son, in Delaware. I found notes that Mary put in my file of papers saying that Jerome told her to call his wife, Clara. Mary never did, as far as I know, and I don't know to this day why she called them in 1986.

May 1986: When I was married, people would call our house asking for *Mary* and I knew they were telemarketers. I didn't like my name being

Mary. I had friends named Mary and I didn't think there was anything wrong with *them* being named Mary, but I didn't like *me* being Mary. I always wished I was officially named Bonnie. So, at the age of 38, with an 8-year-old daughter named Ann, I told my husband that I thought I'd like to look into legally changing my name. Jim understood.

I found out that the process to change one's name required the request be posted in the local newspaper for three weeks in a row, I guess so that if I owed anyone money they had the opportunity to find me. I loved the name Bonnie but never liked the name Susan particularly. No offense to all the Susans I know; you all have lovely names, but I didn't want to be Bonnie Sue. So, what middle name to pick? The cost would be the same for one name change or two. Then in the middle of the night, it came to me. *Ann*! I loved the name Ann, of course! We named my daughter Ann. I would be Bonnie Ann and we would be the first mother/daughter in the history of the world where the mother was named after the daughter.

Later, I told my husband that even if I divorced him I was keeping his last name because all the letters were above the line (very important for cursive writing) and it went so well with "Bonnie."

Sorting through all the papers Mary kept has been eye-opening in many ways. Some things I knew, some I remembered wrong, some were total surprises, all were interesting in that they told me a little more about myself. I don't know why I didn't study these papers in depth years before but "out of sight out of mind" I guess. Now, writing this book and fitting the facts together like a jigsaw puzzle, it's finally all in one place, there to mull over at leisure.

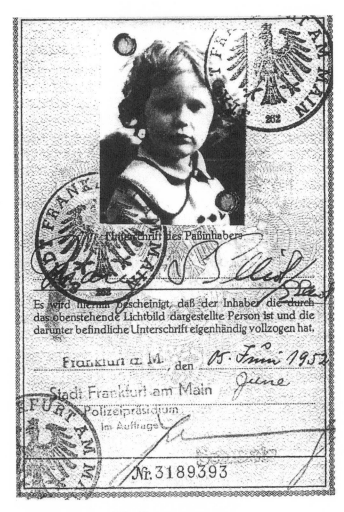

My German passport.

Chapter Sixteen

Growing Up

In 1960 I was 12 years old. Grade school was fun. I liked learning stuff, but the best part of school was recess and the final bell in the afternoon. Every fall I'd start the school year full of expectation, excitement, and energy. By week two, Sister Mary Somebody had already put my name on the board for misbehaving (usually talking to my neighbor) a half dozen times. Every nun had her own system, but somehow I managed to trip each of their triggers.

I now suspect, with good reason because I did the same thing when I was an elementary teacher, that they discussed the troublemakers in their *secret lair lounge* and I'm sure my name came up many times. So, despite my hope that I'd start each year with a clean slate, my reputation preceded me; Mary Spettel chatters too much; Mary Spettel does not have good penmanship; Mary Spettel daydreams; etc, etc, etc.

I graduated from 8th grade in 1962. That summer Mary, Mark and I went to Austria, France, and Germany. We were gone for about three weeks. It was only the second time Mother and Dad had been to Europe. It would not be their last trip.

Even though my parents were older, they were not going to be deterred by having a child in grade school. So, off we went every year on a trip. My mother would tell the teacher to send along some homework. We went on a Caribbean cruise for three weeks in February; Mexico for three weeks one winter, Canada, Florida, California, New York. If they wanted to go, we went. Over the years, after I left the household, they took wonderful, exotic vacations all over the world. I think of their ages then, and how much energy they had, and I marvel at their ability to keep traveling so much and for so long. Riding elephants in India, riding ostriches in Australia, riding donkeys somewhere or other—any chance they had to ride an animal they took it. And I always claimed that they owed their youthfulness to my coming into their lives.

High School was okay. I didn't exactly excel at anything. There were fun times interspersed with having to go to classes and do homework. In the summer between sophomore and junior year, I saw the movie *The Trouble with Angels* with Haley Mills. I became smitten with the idea of boarding school and possibly becoming a nun. I saw myself as Haley in all her antics and adventures. I begged my folks to let me go to Villa Maria Academy in Frontenac, MN (a two-hour drive from La Crosse). Very good friends of my parents had two daughters attending there and I thought those girls were the cat's pajamas.

I felt great envy for their sophisticated mannerism, their ethereal outlook, and their obvious specialness. Well, who can account for perception as a sophomore? My parents agreed to let me enroll. So, was it all I dreamed it would be? NO!! IT WAS NOT! Good Lord, it was like a prison. First of all, 16 girls shared a large dorm with a cubby for our clothes and trundle beds to sleep in. At night we could hear the nuns (they were called Mothers, not Sisters, in the order that ran this dungeon) running a large chain through the double doors to the outside and clicking the padlock.

I guess fire safety rules were not invented back then. The reason they did this was because some of the former girls had taken midnight excursions to the "tower" which was deemed unsafe to be in, especially since old and crazy nuns were locked up in there and there was definitely a ghost or two of nuns that were deemed "not ready for heaven-time." I may be wrong about that last part, but we were young and imaginations ran wild. The first semester would end in mid-January, but I started my "coming home" campaign in November. *Please, please let me come home mid-year. Please don't force me to stay here. Don't you miss me? I miss you. Let's consider this an experiment that went very wrong. I promise I'll do whatever you ask of me, if you just let me go back to Aquinas.* Of course, I realize now that they missed me and wanted me to come home; they were just playing hard to get. In January I rejoined my class and many of my classmates didn't even know I had left. I never again thought about becoming a nun.

As I reflect back on my life, I do not remember anyone every bullying me, or making fun of me, or ridiculing me because I was adopted. I'd like to think that I was perfectly normal and therefore didn't really stand out as someone with a different birth circumstance than anyone else in my friendship circle or my classroom.

I went to the College of St. Teresa in Winona, Minnesota for freshman and sophomore years. I majored in Library Science and minored in English, but secretly I wanted to be an archeologist. The first year I had a room to myself. Being an only child, I didn't think I'd like sharing a room. The only problem was that all the freshmen had to stay in the *old* dorm—Lourdes Hall—and it was beyond scary. It was December before I dared to turn off the light in my room for the night. I had one light (there were no nightlights back then) which was just a lamp on the desk, and that stayed on all night.

There were ghost stories that abounded around the campus. The most notorious of these was The Ghost of Heffern Hall. Even the news, not sure what channel, came there for the anniversary to see if they could film the ghost of the seminarian that had died of fright in the dorm at St. Mary's College—our brother college a mile away. I took German classes at St. Teresa's, but the German Club was at St Mary's and included the gals from St. Teresa's. I would either catch a ride with someone or hitchhike there—always during the daytime—and without worry or fear. *Yup, stupid.*

My English teachers liked me. One nun told me I was a breath of fresh air in her class. I think she just wanted to tell me I was "fresh." My dance teacher loved me. Called me Bonita or "Red." I dyed my hair red the first month I was there. I also started smoking and using terms like "peoples," "Daddio," and "damn" frequently. Boy was I a rebel…without a cause. My grades were tolerable but not spectacular.

I was not in danger of being on the Dean's list, if there even was a Dean's list. I wrote a letter home every other day. I told my parents about my day, my classes, my outside activities, but mostly I just told them what I thought they wanted to hear. Things like, "I'm studying really hard for my World Civics class." "There is a dance tonight at St. Mary's, but I'm going to stay here and play bridge with the girls in the 4th-floor smoker." "We girls are going to the mall to buy school supplies and then stop at the Country Kitchen for some French fries." Never a mention of dates or sleeping right through the alarm for my first class, or getting caught not wearing nylons to class.

I vividly remember our civics teacher. He wore a black eye patch like a pirate. We girls thought that he should run for president because he was so smart and wise. Whenever I hear about kids on campuses today believing their teachers to be infallible—when I hear students wanting to put their instructors on a pedestal—I remember my one-eyed teacher and how foolish our young and impressionable minds were, and how easily he could have led us off a bridge.

After my sophomore year, I moved home, started at the University of Wisconsin La Crosse, but dropped out after half a semester. I just didn't seem to know what I wanted to do and ended up working at the First National Bank. My dad twisted some arms to get me that job. I worked in bookkeeping and transit and I didn't love it. The following year I transferred my credits to Viterbo College in La Crosse and finished my last two years in Elementary Education with a minor in English, Speech, and Drama. My parents pretty much decided my education, my classes, and my future. Education was what they wanted for me, and it would never have occurred to me to contradict them. They knew best, of course. At least that is what I was raised to believe.

Before I graduated, I interned for a semester at Hintgen Elementary in third grade—and I got paid. Then I got my first "real" job working for the University of Wisconsin La Crosse in the recruiting office. I was given a staff car and expenses. I drove all over Wisconsin stopping at high schools, seeing the guidance counselors, and setting up receptions for the seniors where representatives of each department at the university would then show up and try to convince them to attend UW–L.

I was at the university about a year, and then I was hired back to teach in that same grade I interned in at Hintgen. I was there for six years. It was during this time that our first baby died and a year after that I had Ann. After she was born, I did not go back to teaching until she was in first grade.

My dad sold his business, Spettel Office Supply Company, in 1968 (he was 70), which was the year I met Jim. We dated for a year before getting engaged, then waited till we were both done with college before we married. I was a year and a half behind my classmates because of taking time off and because of my intern assignment. Jim was really behind because he took semesters off to ski and tend bar in Boulder, Colorado. But, it was okay. We managed to graduate at the same time, albeit from different schools.

His degree was Business Administration and mine Elementary Education. We were ready to make our mark in the world, or at least in La Crosse. He started his job at Trane Company in Corporate Finance and stayed there until Trane was bought out by American Standard. His job was moved to downtown New York City, where we did not want to live. To this day Ann has never forgiven us for that decision, as she would have loved to be part of the New York scene of ballet and theatre. Oh, well. Life is all about choices.

Our wedding was in April of 1972. My mother was horrified because I didn't give her enough time to plan a really special wedding. I think 4 months was plenty of time. I think she was mostly worried that her friends would assume that I was pregnant and we *had* to get married. Ha, we showed them; I didn't have a baby for five years.

The 29th was a rather chilly, blustery day, but the sun did shine on us during the church service, so that was good. We were both already working at new jobs, so there was no vacation time for us to go on a honeymoon. We went to Rochester, MN (an hour away) for the weekend. The next summer we took our "real" honeymoon, at a lake in Stoughton, Wisconsin owned by Jim's cousin. We had a great time until Jim tried a snap start off the dock on one ski and broke his neck and back. That ended our honeymoon rather abruptly.

Luckily for us, Jim had an instant muscle spasm in his neck and the doctor said that was what probably kept him from severing his spine. He had to stay in the hospital in Stoughton for a week until they built a four-post neck brace for him. Then they sent him home to La Crosse for more treatment. It was many, many months before he healed and many, many more months before we calmed down from that experience. We were probably the youngest couple in history to make a will. Life seemed pretty tenuous for several years. But, time fades all, and it did for this crisis also.

I did not want a full-time teaching position after Ann was born. I actually never expected to go back to teaching at all. But, when Trane got bought out, I decided I'd help out by substitute teaching. And this led, a couple years later, to me applying for a part-time position at the University of Wisconsin La Crosse to supervise student teachers in the field. My experiences working in so many different schools and classrooms and knowing so many teachers and principals in the area schools helped me secure that job. It was fun. I loved working with college students. My job expanded when each year they added more and more responsibility to my contract, and eventually I was full-time.

Ann was a joy to raise. She loved school, loved studying, managed her homework and her outside activities like tennis, poms, singing lessons, Brownies and Girl Scouts, theatre, and ballet with aplomb. She was good at everything she put her mind to. I never had to tell her to pay attention or get her projects done, and her grades were always great. I'm not sure who she took after, but I can assure you that it was not me as far as studies went. Jim and she are much alike—single-minded in their determination to get a project finished, vigorous in getting all the information correct and completed, and presenting their best foot forward. I'm kind of an *okay, here it is, hope it's what you wanted, and if it isn't, please don't make me do it again* person. So, despite her mother, Ann turned into a lovely young woman, a perfect employee, a great wife, and a wonderful mother. She makes her dad and me very proud.

In November of 1990 my adoptive father, Mark, passed away. He was 92. He had had a good life—mostly healthy— although the last couple years he had dementia, and part of his last year he was in a nursing home. Mother decided she wanted to bring him home and provide 24-hour care for him. She was a determined woman who fought the nursing home staff, who felt he would be better in their facility. It was not always easy, and sometimes a caregiver wasn't able to show up and I had to go over and take an eight-hour shift. It was hard; working, raising Ann, having Jim working in a different city (Milwaukee) after Trane Company restructured, and helping my dad and mother.

Mother needed a lot of help after her husband of 67 years was gone. They were so close and needed each other, and when he was not there she fell apart. Within a couple years she needed to go to a nursing home also. It was a wonderful facility and she was there for six years; they treated her like a queen.

Once Ann went to college, she didn't need me anymore, and that was fine. It was while I was working at the university that we traveled to Green Valley, AZ two years in a row to visit friends and ended up buying property in early April of 2000, just a week before my brother first contacted me and a couple weeks before our 38th wedding anniversary.

I continued to work at the university (for 16 years) and Jim, who had already retired, spent time in Arizona so he could oversee the construction of our winter home. He stayed in Tucson with his brother, David, who had a construction management company and had lived all over the world, usually for 2 to 4 years at a time while he made sure that whatever project he was hired for was completed correctly and on time. I would fly down to Green Valley fairly often to visit because David's wife was a flight attendant for American Airlines and would give me passes. I didn't retire for another three years, but eventually I decided I wanted to spend my winters in warm and sunny Arizona, too. It was hard to leave the university because I still loved my job, but, it was time. That was 2004.

Our wedding in 1972.

Our daughter, Ann,
at 2 weeks old.

My dad loved Ann
so much.

Who's taller? My dad
was pretty short at 5' 6"

One of my two
horses, Topper.

1961

Chapter Seventeen

1998—A Stranger's Help

I promised my daughter I'd find my birth family. For my sake and hers, we needed medical information. As I approached my 50th birthday, I asked her if she'd like to take a trip with me (my husband was busy running his business and would not be going with us) to somewhere—anywhere. Her answer: "Mom, let's go find your birth family." Oh boy! One big problem: my birth family *probably* lived in East Berlin. So many questions had been unanswered about my origins. My birth certificate held no information about what time of day I was born. I didn't know my birth weight or height. It did list a hospital name.

Did my birth mother hold me for a few minutes and say goodbye? Was her husband there with her? Was he angry? Was she embarrassed because she'd had an affair? Did they want to get this inconvenience over with quickly and get back to their lives and any other children? Would any of these questions be answered if I found them? Would she be happy to see me? Would her husband demand I stay away? Would I find out who my birth father was? Did she know? Would she tell? Was he an American soldier? Ann and I did celebrate my birthday in Europe. We went to Prague, Vienna, and Budapest and had a lovely trip, but it had nothing to do with finding my birth family. There was no time to do that before I turned 50.

My birth certificate said I was born in an area known as Lichtenberg, a section of Berlin that went to Russia after WWII. I realized that I needed to concentrate on those unanswered questions in my life and that I needed to do some research. I did not speak German well enough to be making phone calls or writing to government officials asking for information. Plus, I had read that Germany was very protective of the birth parents' right to privacy.

I needed to get over my fear of failing and my fear of *finding*. In all those years, no one from Germany had tried to find me, at least as far as I knew. *Was my birth mother dead? Did she ever wonder what happened to me? Did she really have other children as Dorothy suggested to me in her letter? Mary said Dorothy gave her the impression that my father was not Erika's husband. That was all I knew.*

I started with the Church of Latter Day Saints, hoping I could check records there – that was a dead end – the people I was searching for were not old enough. I did learn about the International Soundex Reunion Registry from them. A person lists their name and all the information they have about their adoption and hope that someone is looking for them and has also registered. You could only register if you were 18. I was told that there was no one matching my search parameters, but I should leave my name on the site and hope someone would eventually check it.

I called the German Consulate in Chicago. Could they help me in any way? The man I spoke with was not interested in helping me because I was no longer a German citizen. I looked up private detectives in La Crosse. The one I spoke to said it would be rare for a private detective to be able to work internationally, especially without speaking the language, and that hiring a go-between might be quite expensive. I thought of flying to Berlin and finding a private detective there who spoke English, but I hated to get there and then end up with no information.

I went to our local library and looked in the Minneapolis, Minnesota yellow pages to see if someone might have advertised that they knew how to do an international search for a birth family and I did find someone who specialized in German adoptions. I wrote to him and he wrote back saying that he would need my social security number and birth dates and copies of my birth records and power of attorney to make inquiries on my behalf. My husband said absolutely not! We were not giving him any power of attorney.

Back at the library, the research librarian suggested the archives room where I ended up spending hours and hours. Nothing could be checked out of that room, so I took copious notes. Eventually, I came across a small publication called *Geboren Deutscher (Born German)*. It was a 9 X 12 newsletter written by a man who had been searching for his German birth mother for years. During his journey he encountered many people with similar stories; they were either looking for birth parents, finding birth parents, being disappointed after finding birth parents or finding children given up for adoption. I read story after story of how the search and the encounter and the aftermath went. Some were good stories with happy endings; *most* were not. It worried me to think my story would not have a happy ending, but I was committed to continuing my search.

In this newsletter, I noticed that many of the storytellers credited a woman named Leonie Boehmer with helping them find their families. Within the newsletter, she had an advertisement saying she helped reunite birth families in Germany, Austria, and Switzerland. And miracle of miracles, she listed an email address and I wrote an email to her.

I explained the circumstances of my birth and told her about the man from Minneapolis who wanted too much personal information, and that my husband would not allow that. I asked her what she charged for her services. "I am 50 years old now and I guess I just feel I should put some closure to this long open book of my life." I ended my email to her by saying: "I have put this off for so long. When you just live with possibilities, they can be anything. Reality is harder to deal with, e.g. that my birth mother is not waiting for me to contact her because she is long dead and her secrets died with her." I told Leonie that I was baptized in an army barracks and perhaps my father was an American soldier. Unless my mother was alive there might be no way to trace him.

The very next day I received an email back from Leonie. She said she had found her own daughter whom she had given up for adoption in 1957, and she mentioned how close she and her daughter's adoptive parents had become. Leonie retired from her career in 1991 and devoted her time to helping German-born adoptees and their German birth parents find one another. She was president of her local chapter of Operation Identity. She had been a certified independent search consultant since 1983. Interestingly, she immigrated to the United States the same year I did.

She did indeed need my SSN and I would have to have some papers notarized so she could sign my name to documents she would be requesting. She told me that if I wished to do the search myself, she would be happy to provide the address for the registration office in Berlin so they could tell me if my mother was still alive or was deceased. She admonished me to not mention that my inquiry was regarding *adoption*. She said it was difficult dealing with the German authorities because they do not like adoptees contacting them, so she never mentioned that she was searching for adoption reasons.

She also said that the German authorities would not give out information on any siblings, living or dead, if the parents were already deceased. If that was the case, she thought we might be able to go through a probate court. I knew that there was no way I wanted to deal with all that confusing paperwork on my own. I was still not sure if my husband would allow me to give her this information or let me sign any papers. It's not like today when you give your SSN to every Tom, Dick and IRS agent. Jim agreed that it was the only way I was ever going to be able to proceed with my search, and I hired her.

And so it began. I signed the necessary paperwork to allow Leonie to inquire at the proper government offices in Berlin on my behalf. I knew I could never move forward as quickly or as easily as she could. Leonie did not charge for her services; she only asked to be reimbursed for postage and payments for copies of documents. I had to give Leonie permission to sign my name, and also to allow all letters and documents from Germany to go to her address. I had to send all the pertinent paperwork to her so she could figure out where to start the search. She only asked for an initial $25 to get started. I sent her $100. She promised that she would send me all original paperwork and her translations.

On June 10, 1999, she wrote to the registration office in Berlin. She pretended to be me. *"Dear Madams and Sirs! For some time I have been searching for my mother who lived in Berlin, Lichtenberg, Atzpodienstr. 30 in 1948. Her name is Erika Gerda Irene Paul née Müller. Her husband's name was Gerhard Benno Hermann Paul. Would you please be so kind and provide me with her present address? Enclosed is $10.00 for the charges. Sincerely, Mary Susan Spettel aka Bonnie Willemssen."* She added her address to the bottom.

It had started. My search had officially started. I was maybe going to find out who my family was. I was excited, but very worried that it would not turn out the way I had dreamed it would. Would we find them? Would they want to know me? Would they even speak to me? What would I do if they rejected me? One thing I knew for sure, I was finally doing something instead of just wondering.

Chapter Eighteen

1999—2000 A Year of Correspondence

A nd so a year of correspondence with Leonie began. In an early e-mail I wrote, *"I know I will have to accept whatever the past has carved out for me. For so long I didn't have a burning desire to seek out my birth family, perhaps because I always knew I was adopted and because I thought my adoptive parents might be hurt by my search. My father has now been deceased for ten years and my mother is 95 and in a nursing home. My twenty-year-old daughter is the one who has been trying to get me to do this search."*

Leonie mentioned the International Soundex Reunion Registry and I told her I'd filled out the forms for that already with no results, but she had me fill it out again. It's a confidential form that people fill out hoping to connect with family that might be looking for them. You put in as much information as you might have and hope that someone else has that same information. I had very little information, but I had my birth mother's name, my birth name, and the city my birth mother lived in. Leonie translated it into German and made sure it was distributed at the German adoption agencies and support groups. I never got "a hit" from circulating that form. But, I understand it works for many people.

It wasn't until October 18, 1999, (five months after contacting Leonie) that I wrote again and asked her if she had ever received an answer to her

June letter. *Did I sit around in those months dying to know what was going on? No. I only fleetingly thought about it.* Leonie answered and said that the wheels turned slowly, but she would send a follow up letter to Germany. More time passed. When I didn't hear from Leonie I would basically forget about my search. Then she would email about some new lead and I would again be nervous about the outcome of my quest.

I sent Leonie some letters and documents that had been written and signed by the husband of my birth mother. She sent me the translation of those papers in which Gerhard Paul stated he was the *legal* father of the child known as Gerda Erika Paul. Leonie said that after doing the translation, it seemed to her that he was really my birth father. He did not deny paternity. *I didn't believe her. I was sure I knew the correct story; I was the product of an affair. He was just 'saving face' for his wife.*

On November 3, 1999, Leonie wrote an email informing me that she had received information, finally, and it was that my birth mother had died in September 1983. She expressed her deepest sympathy. *Even though it had been 16 years since my mother had died, at that moment, for me, she had died right then.* I sat at the computer and cried. Jim came home a short time later and found me sobbing. I told him what Leonie had learned. He said, "Your mother died in 1983, that's so long ago."

"No," I told him, "For me she died today." And, bless him, he understood, or at least tried to be supportive. *I had always feared I would not ever get to meet her. By not searching for her I could just pretend that she was alive and looking for me.*

Leonie then wrote to the Vital Statistics Office in Berlin and said that I (she, of course) would like a copy of the death certificate and she enclosed $10.00 (*what else?*) for postage and handling. She also asked them to send the address for the probate court so that I/she could find next of kin.

In 1983 (when my birth mother died) my daughter was only five. My adoptive folks were quite elderly by then. My dad was slowly falling into dementia and my mother was overwhelmed with caretaking issues. The Berlin Wall was still up. I most certainly would not have tried to trace my heritage at that time. *Did my birth mother wonder why I didn't try to contact her when I was 18 or 21? Or did she live in fear that someday I would show up at her door?* I know now that she never told anyone except her close first cousin, Sophie, what had happened to her. *I looked back at my calendar on September 11, 1983. What was I doing that day? But that square was blank. No lunches, no trips, no interesting pastime that would have coincided with her dying in Berlin that day. Of course, years later 9/11 had its own special significance.*

"Dear Leonie. Well it is certainly sad news and I've had my cry, but I guess I didn't hold out a lot of hope that my mother was still alive—just a small glimmer. My desire now is that you might find some relatives. Wow, after 51 years of wondering, I finally know something. So, keep digging for me, please. There is much yet to know about my heritage, and hopefully about my family medical history."

Leonie wrote again to the Vital Statistics Office in Berlin requesting a copy of Erika's death certificate and enclosing another $10.00. After much paperwork back and forth from Berlin to New Mexico (Leonie's home) I zoned out of the birth family search and concentrated on my life in Wisconsin. By December, Leonie had a copy of Erika's death certificate and Erika's husband's death certificate. On it I discovered that my birth mother was born on October 31, 1914—Halloween in the U.S.

The death certificate for Gerhard Benno Hermann Paul said he died on December 27, 1977. He was born October 15, 1905. I was not particularly interested in this information. After all, I *knew* he was not my father. Why would they give me up for adoption otherwise? She must have had an affair. *I daydreamed about whom my father might be; a soldier, a baker, a prince?*

As a child, I worried so much about my adoptive parents dying before I was able to take care of myself. It's scary when you are 8 or 10 and you think your parents are ancient. They were much older than my friends' parents. Mark was born in 1898 and Mary was born in 1903. Now, through this search, I found out my birth mother was already 34 when she had me and her husband, Gerhard, was only two years younger than my adoptive mother, Mary. *If I had been raised in Berlin would his age have mattered to me as much?*

An email from Leonie dated March 22, 2000, said, "I am amazed, but on the copy of the will that came today, written in 1970, it lists all your siblings and their addresses as of 1983." Apparently, in all her years of doing searches, Leonie had never had the probate court send a copy of the back of the will listing names of the inheritors. She thinks this happened because on my birth certificate it does not say that I was adopted. Adopted children in Germany have no right to information or money. For me, it was the pivotal point to finding my birth family.

Leonie continued, "On the Internet I found only one of the heirs still at the address from 17 years ago—your sister, Helga. I could not find the boys. Maybe you could get through to your sister." Leonie listed the names of my siblings—Helga (1934), Dietrich (1939), Detlaf (1943), and Klaus (1936) (who was excluded from the will with no reason given). Later, I found out Klaus had run away from home when he was 17 and his father had never forgiven him or knew his whereabouts.

At first I asked Leonie to call Helga and ask her my many questions. But Leonie wrote and said, "That's not how it's done. You have to write a letter and send it to me and I'll translate it and send it on." She told me to write to my sister and enclose some pictures. That was March 23rd and it took me until April 11th to get that unbelievably difficult letter written. I mailed it to Leonie and she told me not to expect any reply for at least a month because of the slowness of the postal service. In my letter to my sister—half-sister?—I asked for medical information and I told her a little about myself, but not a lot because I wasn't sure if she would even be interested. I enclosed a picture and a copy of some of the papers I possessed about my birth. I asked her if she knew who my birth father was.

Leonie wrote to me after she translated my letter and told me that Gerhard Paul was my father because he stated as much in the letter he wrote, and he was listed on my birth certificate as the father. Again, I didn't believe she was correct. Dorothy had hinted to Mary and Mark that they would be "surprised" at who my father was. She told me, in that letter I received in high school, that she was sure that I had older half-siblings. That was all I had to go on. *I guess I would rather believe that my birth mother had an affair than contemplate that my birth parents gave me up for some reason.*

Here is part of my letter, written on April 13, 2000.

"Hello Helga,

This might come as a surprise to you. I am your sister...your half-sister. I have been trying to find my birth family for about a year now. Through the help of a wonderful woman named Leonie Boehmer, I was able to locate you through our mother's death certificate. I imagine you must remember me because you and my half-brothers are all older than I am, so you must remember our mother carrying me and the time when she decided she had to give me up for adoption. I am not bitter or regretful about that act on her part. I'm sure she did what she had to do...what she thought was the best thing for everyone at the time....I would love to get to know you and my brothers a little better. I am, of course, very curious about our mother...and wonder too if you know who my father might have been? I was adopted twice—once right after birth and then again when I was four.

My first adoptive mother could no longer care for me and an American family—older people who could not have children of their own—adopted me. I have grown up in Wisconsin....I am married to a wonderful man named Jim and we have one daughter named Ann who is 21 years old....I am enclosing a picture so you can get to know me a little better. I would love to see some pictures of you and my brothers, and of course our mother....and of course to find out more about health history for myself and for my daughter....I enclosed some official papers to prove to you who I am and you will see that with the information I already had, it wasn't too terribly difficult to finally locate you.... if you are interested in ever meeting face-to-face, I would love to fly to Germany and meet you......do you speak English? My German isn't too good. Aber Ich spreche ein bisschen Deutch....goodbye for now. It would mean the world to me if you would write. Fondly, your sister Bonnie Willemssen (born: Gerda Erika Paul).

Leonie warned me that a letter to Germany takes at least 10 days. "Do not expect to hear anything for four weeks." Again, she stated that she was positive that Gerhard Benno Herman Paul was my birth father. I still doubted it. I thought he just said it so that it would be easier for my mother to sign papers to give me up and not embarrass herself by listing a different name for my real father. Leonie translated my letter and sent it to Berlin on April 20, 2000. I tried to forget about it because every other letter had taken so long to get results. However, in only seven days (April 27, 2000) I was speaking to one of my brothers (Dietrich) and to my sister for the first time in my life.

My initial e-mail to Leonie went out on April 25, 1999; my brother's call to me was April 27, 2000—one year and two days later. A lot of paperwork traveled across the Atlantic, a lot of emails pulsed through the air, a lot of tears, a lot of smiles, a lot of firsts.

Picture I enclosed with my first letter to Helga in 2000.

Chapter Nineteen

Summertime, and the Living Was (sort of) Easy

I had found my birth family. I was communicating with them. Ann was getting to know her first cousin through emails. Even Jim was getting to know my brothers, especially Klaus who called him "Cowboy Jimmy" and wanted to know if he had a horse and a gun. I'm not sure just what Klaus thought America was like, but it was cute. He would sometimes say, during our many phone calls, "Will Cowboy Jimmy shoot me because we didn't come and find you?" I would say, "No, Klaus, he understands that none of you knew I existed."

I let Dieter pick out the best time for me to visit them in Berlin and somehow it became September 5th—Labor Day. It was the best time for him as he was still working at the airlines and he always had five days on and five days off. I would arrive when he had five days off. Because I was staying for two weeks, he would have to go back to work while I was there.

Unfortunately, it was terrible timing for me. I would have preferred visiting in July or August when it wouldn't interfere with my teaching schedule at the university. I had to ask my boss, "Would you be willing to let me miss the first two weeks of school?" Once she heard my reason, she was very generous and even offered to teach my classes for me for those two weeks. But settled in theory was not settled in my mind. I had a lot of preparation to do for my classes and was teaching a new subject that semester. On top of that, Jim's annual family reunion (a week in Maine) was planned for the middle of August. *As I spent every free minute I could organizing my materials for my classes (which I would start the day after returning from Germany) I never imagined how different I'd be; how changed my life would be after meeting my siblings.*

Flying to Germany by myself was something I chose to do. Ann was beginning her semester at Oberlin. Jim could have come with me, but I knew that if he did there would not be room to stay with Dieter and something deep inside me said I would learn so much more by staying right there in my brother's apartment. I made the right decision, but it was so hard to say goodbye to Jim the morning my plane left. I cried and clung to him for dear life. I was flying so far, and so alone. I was going to another world, one where most of the people surrounding me would not speak my language, and where I would have to be totally responsible for myself. It was very scary.

But, I realized that there were people eager to meet me—three brothers and a sister and a niece and sister-in-law who were so excited that I would soon be plunging into their world.

My very first letter from Dieter, after our first couple conversations, started out, *"Welcome to our family. We are looking forward very much to become acquainted with you and yours and we are longing for the day when we can embrace you and clasp you in our arms."* Can you imagine reading those words? This was my first correspondence from *my brother.* I was in 7ᵗʰ Heaven.

Dieter had looked for a long time, and finally found our brother, Klaus, living in Frankfurt-an-Main. Dieter had help from the *Deutsches Rotes Kreuz* (German Red Cross) in about 1990. He had not seen him since 1954 when Klaus ran away from home because their father beat him. For some reason (Dieter said it was because Gerhard felt Klaus was lazy) Gerhard was harder on Klaus than the others. Gerhard was a very strict, military type of father. Klaus got fed up with his treatment and ran away from home. By the age of 18 he was married with twin daughters and was living in Frankfurt-an-Main.

Dieter said that Detti was a "bit of an eccentric and we cannot identify with his way of living." Detti married three times, fathered five children, and was a house painter when he was not drinking too much. He expected people to take care of him, and his wives and girlfriends did just that. The woman he was living with, in her apartment, when I met him, was 15 years his senior.

It was in that letter that Dieter said he had a *"very heartfelt relation to our mother and with Dad I made peace when he got older. I very respected my parents. After Papa's death at X-mas of 1977, Mum stayed alive for six years. She made trips around with contemporaries and to hen parties a.s.o. (he means "and so on"). When Eszter laid in childbed with Ramona, Mum also laid at the same time in the same hospital suffering from breast cancer. She also had surgeries for cataracts and she had glaucoma. She was almost blind, but after the eye-operation she could see again using special glasses. It is a pity, when Papa died Ramona was only seven months old, so she could not know her grandpa. But to Grandma she had a very tender relation. Ramona was grandma's darling. Mum coddled her from top to bottom.*

Alas, as the doctors say, the chance to survive a cancer-operation is about 6 years. And so it went. For God's sake, Mum could be to Ramona a lovely grandma for six years. Well, I must say our daughter was in particular very well-behaved and pretty as a child. We never had troubles with her. She always smiled to everyone, played also without playmates. Where we placed her down, there she remained."

Dieter said that Mama's cancer came back and was inoperable. She got chemo and lost her hair and had to walk with crutches, yet she would go to Helga's in West Berlin and climb to the 4th floor each week. Later she got injections for morphine. Everyone visited her every day, but the doctors (called professors in Germany) made them go home. Whenever Erika would wake up, she would ask Dieter if it was Sunday yet because she was born on a Sunday. Dieter said that he, Eszter, and Ramona also were born on a Sunday, which meant you would have a good life. Erika wanted to die on a Sunday, and she did, early in the morning on September 11, 1982.

Dieter described their apartment. *"We live in a little three-room flat on the 2nd floor. Our flat by German standards is medium sized, but by American standards, small. When you come to us, Ramona will leave you her room to sleep."* He talked about their "garden house," built in 1982.

He was interested in whether Ann played an instrument. He said she should have "musical roots". *"I ask therefore, because we are a bit of musicians in our family. Klaus played always from his youth the accordion very good. Papa played too, always at birthday parties. I played accordion and guitar full-timed in the sixties as a member of a 3-man band and I sang besides. Ramona took music lessons in accordion for six years. Mum also played the accordion during the war.*

My English knowledge I learned from trips and my job. I know a lot of vocabularies but speaking fluently is a bit hard for me especially on the telephone. Ramona speaks more fluent, but if I write, I can think over what I like to say. If you are here and we talked about one or two ours, you will hear a flood of words like a waterfall from me. Lovely greetings, dear sister."

Dieter ended this first letter by apologizing for writing so much. *Like that would be a problem for me, who hungered for any information I could possibly get.* "I wrote everything that came to my mind," he said. "We are waiting very much for our first meeting. I have a good feeling and I believe everything works out in a nice way between us."

Chapter Twenty

My Bonnie Lies Over the Ocean

Over the next few months we kept the post office in business. Letters flew back and forth, most accompanied by pictures or copies of pictures. One problem for me, however, was that I was writing in English and they were writing in German. My brother Klaus worked for a limousine company in Frankfurt and learned to speak a modicum of English while transporting tourists and business people to their destinations, so his letters were interspersed with English words.

Dieter was my second youngest brother. His first letter to me, which included many photos, never arrived. The photos were copies, thank Heaven. He wrote again, all in English, and re-sent the photos. I'm sure Ramona helped him with it. He had to use English in his job at Aeroflot and later, after the Berlin Wall came down, at Lufthansa. *Can you imagine what it was like to open a letter from someone you are related to but have never known?*

In the letter he told me about meeting his wife, Eszter, at Lake Balaton while he was on holiday in Hungary. A year later they were married. When they met, neither spoke the other's language, but Dieter had a knack for languages and learned hers quickly. In 2000 they were celebrating their silver anniversary.

"We are a merry and vivacious family, sometimes we are brawling, too. Because of Eszter's Hungarian temperament, we have sometimes a bit louder disputes. Ramona is "half and half" meaning she is a citizen of Hungary and Germany and has two passports. We are in character a bit Hungarian, eat Hungarian food, and have a bit of Hungarian mode of living." I found out later that it was 20 years before Eszter was allowed to become a German citizen. *"Since the "Wall of Shame" broke down, we made many trips abroad to take advantage of the cheaper plane tickets while I still work for Lufthansa."*

Because he worked for Globe Ground Berlin, a subsidiary of Lufthansa, they could all fly standby for about 10% of the cost, and they had been to the Netherlands, Spain, Thailand, Cypress, Africa, Bali, Barbados, Jamaica, Antigua, Greece and many trips to Hungary and to Arizona, California, Nevada, and Florida. He had worked from 1965 to 1991 as an aircraft *"mechanician"* and from 1991 to 2000 as ground staff for servicing the aircraft. Here is where we differed: I hated to fly, and he *loved* to fly.

Dieter continued by telling me how he had been frustrated trying to trace me in Berlin using the paperwork I had sent him. The bureau would not give him a copy of my German birth certificate without a proxy from me and certification by a lawyer. He said, *"Bonnie, dear sister, you must believe me, I really want to help you find your biological father. When you are here I will take you to all the important places, like your birthplace, our former flat, and the cemeteries and to meet aunts and uncles."*

In my first contact letter to them, when I had asked if they had any medical information that I could pass along to my daughter and I found out about my mother's breast cancer, that alone made the search worthwhile. Dieter said that his father, Gerhard, had died of colon cancer, but sad as that was for them, it didn't mean much to me at the time. I found out that the government allowed the elderly free access to West Berlin in hopes that they would not come back to East Berlin to live and continue to be a burden on Russia's finances. Dieter also told me he visited with Helga, the oldest, every week. He and Detti, the youngest, who lived only 20 minutes from Dieter, were not on speaking terms at that time.

Soon I would be talking to my brothers and my sister in person. *What would it be like to see them? How in the world would it ever make up for so much lost time? Was that even the goal? Perhaps just starting from this point in time was all we could do.*

Chapter Twenty–One

Thank God For Computers

In that last month before I flew to Berlin to meet my family, Ramona and I continued to email several times a week. She told me that Gerhard, Erika's husband, fought for the Nazis (at the time it was the only German military). Dieter told me they all hated the Nazis, but if you refused to join you were *"dropped into a prison or killed"*. Ramona said she didn't know if her Grandma and Grandpa believed in Hitler, but *"this was the problem with Germany at the time, one takes the power in his hand and the others do as he wants. Thank God these days are over although there are a few stupid people called Neo-Nazis and a lot of West German people don't like the "Easties," but I don't care, I don't need to communicate with those people."*

Ramona could only check her computer at work or at the university; she had many exams to study for and worked hard. In between, she was trying to help her dad communicate with me. She did a lot of translating in both directions. She did compliment my German when I sent gifts and cards and letters and wrote them in German. I used the German dictionary frequently, but my two years of German in high school and my two years of German in college and several trips to Germany helped a lot.

My brother Klaus was not told about me finding them until mid-May of 2000. Ramona said, *"...we told him the news and he was very surprised and maybe a bit shocked. I don't know if he really catched what my dad said. Maybe he needs some more days to recognize everything. Detti doesn't know yet. He will be with Helga on Saturday and she will tell him."*

On July 5, 2000 I wrote a letter, in German, to my brothers Detti and Klaus. I had not spoken in person or by letter to either of them yet and I wanted to make a connection. Here is what I wrote, using my electronic German translator.

"Liebe Bruder Klaus und Detti, Heir ist dein Schwester, Bonnie. Du bis uberraschen zu lernen um mich. Ich habe gewartet bis Ich funfzig Jahre alt war, bevor Ich meine Familie gesucht hat. Ich sollte vor zehn Jarhre angefangen, oder bevor Mama gestroben ist. Ich kann nicht auf Deutsch sagen alles Ich brauchen zu sagen. Ich hoffe das Du ein Freund hast der das Englisch sprechen kann. Und Ich habe ein Deutsch Tutor. Es ist nicht zu gut, aber Ich kann spreche ein bischken. Ich sprach mit Helga fur 40 minuten vor ein paar Woche. Dieter kann Englisch sprechen so es ist nicht schwer. Ramona sprecht gut Englisch. Wir kann 'e-mail' zu einander. Hast du 'e-mail?' Bitte, schreib mich einer Brief. Ich habe meine Tutor zu ubersetzen. Mein leben ish sehr gut, aber Ich wollte Mama kennenlernen. Anbei ist mein Baby Bild und den Brief Ich an Ramona und Dieter und Helga geschicht habe. Auf Wiedersehen. Meine Gramarik ist schelect. Sehr oft muss Ich Worter in Worterbuch nachschlagen. Ich komme am 5.Sept. an und fleige am 19.Sept.ab. Ich freue mich aft meine Reise. Kommst Du nach Berlin, oder soll Ich mit dem Zug nach Frankfurt reisen, Klaus? Ich habe Frankfurt zweimal besucht, und Ich habe Berlin einmal besucht. Ich begrusse Dich. Deine "kleine' Schwester, Bonnie."

The first letter my oldest brother Klaus sent to me I had translated by a friend/neighbor.

It said, *"Dear Bonnie, thank you for the letter you sent. I have read and looked at everything with great interest. You can believe I was very surprised to learn of your existence. All these years without knowing of a second sister that wasn't with us. I cannot walk you through my entire life history right now but I will give you a little resume. From the era of 1936 until 1947 I was a happy, uncomplaining kid. The time was nice, although turbulent. We were twice evacuated for safety up to 1945. But, then, our father from the (French) prison camp came home and my happy childhood was gone. He beat me a lot and I didn't know why. There was no loving words, no love, no trust, only strict rules. In 1954, when I was 17, and because of the way father was, I went over the border illegally to West Berlin. I have never gone back. It was a struggle for existence which I lost. I never had a nice life. I am an old (64) sick man that has nothing and is nothing. As I think about it, I would have gladly exchanged places with you but everybody has their own fate."* The letter was long and I learned so much about him. Klaus was my goofy brother, the one who joked and made faces and laughed all the time. *He was a lot like me.*

My first letter from Helga was dated May 2, 2000. The smell of cigarette smoke lingered heavily on the pages. Helga was also an avid beer drinker. She wrote that she thought that my baby pictures looked like her papa: *"Perhaps my father is your father."* When I visited Berlin in September I told them that I would like to do DNA testing, but Helga got very angry when she heard that. She told Dieter that there was no need for DNA testing, that we were all brothers and sisters. I don't know if she was just hoping that it was true or upset that our mother could have had an affair. Months later, after the tests came back declaring it 99.95% positive that we were *full* brothers and sisters, hers was the first excited voice I heard on my voice mail about it. We did the test in both Germany and Wisconsin and Dieter got the results a day before I did. He told Helga and she called me. Not that I could understand what she was saying, but I got the idea.

Helga and Detti and Klaus and Dieter did not have computers and therefore no email to and from. I was so lucky that Ramona was at university and had email there. She had a computer at their apartment also, but wrote off-line and then connected only to push "send" and then went off-line again to save money. Ramona had internet installed in their apartment that summer so we could email more easily. She hoped we had Microsoft Word '97. *Boy, was that a long time ago.*

"Dear Ramona, I think about all of you constantly. I am still in such a daze thinking of this miracle. It is so marvelous. I was wondering if Dieter or someone knows where my mother might have worked in 1947. That might give us a little clue as to who my father might have been. Also, did you say that I have two aunts and an uncle? I can't wait to hear all about relatives. I

promised you that I would start the story of how I got to America. I won't do too much all at once because it's a long story. So, here goes:"

And with that, I wrote about my adoptions and my life up to finding them in April of 2000, telling my life story, which I pared down to a few hundred words. Ramona wrote an email saying, *"I am looking forward to the next part of your life story. You stopped when it was the most exciting part. My parents said it is like a book, the first chapter we finished and we like to read more....we are very excited and like to know everything about you in only one day, which is impossible, I know. I am looking forward to meet you personally soooooo much. Lovingly, your niece Ramona."*

Typical emails between Ramona and me were similar to this: *"We can't wait your coming. I hope your plane reservation will match. If Dad has to work, no problem, I will come to the airport to catch you....I hope you have the package we sent you with more pictures and a small thing for everyone. I don't like to tell you what, because the surprise will be gone.... I am so sorry, you don't even know how we look like....I have so much to do for now, I don't know "where my head is standing" as the Germans say."*

Ramona continued, *"I called a few minutes ago to wish happy birthday to Helga because in Germany, they say, it brings the whole year unluck, when you gratulate before the official day."*

For my birthday Dieter wrote, *"Only 35 more days till we can embrace each other. We are very waiting for your coming. Most of the time Eszter will be cooking Hungarian food, sometimes German food, too, but we like the Hungarian more."*

In July, Ramona was still asking me if I had received any packages from them. They had sent pictures. We didn't have Facebook then; we didn't have cell phones, or cell phones with cameras on them to allow us to text photos back and forth. I didn't know what my family looked like. I had sent them some pictures so they knew what we looked like. Ramona said I looked a lot like her. Klaus looked the most like our mother and we discovered later that I looked the most like our father. By mid-July, Ramona said that they were sure the package was lost and they were going to trace it. By August (three months after our first conversation) I finally was able to open an attachment that Ramona sent to my computer and see what they looked like. It was so wonderful, searching those faces for similarities to mine.

*My time to visit was fast approaching. I was scared and excited and nervous and joyful and **really** scared. I worried about everything. What clothes should I pack? Did they dress up? What time did they get up in the morning? Would I like my sister-in-law's Hungarian food? What would it be like to share a two-bedroom one-bathroom apartment with total strangers? Would I be able to manage the steps to Helga's 4th-floor apartment? Would I be too hot? Too cold? Would they like me? Would I like them? What would I find out that would change me to the core?*

Dieter wrote now and then; not as often as Ramona. On my 52nd birthday, I actually spoke with each of my four siblings, even Detti whom I had never before heard on the phone. It was amazing. Surreal.

Ramona answered my questions when she could. I asked why they never fled from East Berlin. Here is her explanation.

"Dad always wanted to leave East Germany. He always dreamt of a life in America or Hawaii when he was young; later my parents thought about leaving to live in Budapest because life was a bit better there in the eastern times. We never had a bad life; the only problem was that it was not allowed to travel to western countries. Berlin, as the capital of the GDR, had always enough to eat, although I think it was another thing in the villages."

We sent gifts back and forth; mostly souvenirs of our respective hobbies and countries. I found out my sister collected turtles. *Turtles! I couldn't believe it. So did I. I loved turtles. How could we both have an affinity for them?* After a while we decided it was getting too expensive to be mailing packages overseas. I was sending to four people, which made it even more expensive. A German tradition I learned about when I visited was the showering of little gifts when visiting someone in their home. Each time my brother and I would visit Helga he would bring along flowers or some little gift, even if we were just stopping in for tea and we had just been there the day before.

Another custom is to kiss on both cheeks each time you meet, or at the very least on one cheek. If you officially belong to a church in Germany, you must pay 5 or 10 percent of your salary to the state automatically. It's why Dieter and family did not join any church. But, he said they went to church on Christmas and Easter. On Sundays, it's forbidden to mow the lawn between 1 and 3 in the afternoon. I learned so much about customs in Germany.

I was unprepared for the tradition, especially religious tradition, which dominated Germany. Stores all closed on Sundays, bringing gifts each time you visited someone, taking off your shoes each time you entered an apartment or house. America seemed very informal and somewhat frivolous after being with my new family.

First photo I received to see what my birth family looked like -
my sister-in-law, Eszter and my niece, Ramona.

Another photo they sent. My brother, Dieter,
and my niece in Trinidad in 1993.

Chapter Twenty–Two

Flying To Meet My Family

As the plane took off in September of 2000, I watched the tarmac. My heart was in La Crosse, but my thoughts were in Berlin. I could feel the lift of the plane's body, the engines revving frantically to get all our combined weights off the ground. Here I was, 52 years of age, flying to Germany alone to meet my siblings for the very first time. Helga, the oldest was 66; Klaus was 64, Dieter 61, and Detti 57. Ramona was 23 at this time.

I let my head fall back on the headrest, dreading the long flight yet in some ways hoping it would never end. The people waiting for me were strangers. *Why in the world did I open this can of worms?*

The man in the seat next to me commented on the smooth takeoff. I forced my agreement through clenched teeth, as I'm a nervous flyer. "Where are you headed?" he asked. We were going to be seatmates for the next nine hours.

"Berlin," I responded, only slightly less nervous now that we were in the air than I had been ten minutes earlier.

"Business or pleasure?"

"I'm going to visit my sister and my brothers," I answered, again feeling that surreal aura that came over me each time I spoke those words out loud.

"Oh, has it been a long time since you've seen them?" he continued.

"Eons," I returned, secretly smiling at my little white lie. I was not going to tell a stranger on the plane my life story, but now, 18 years later, I'm doing exactly that.

The flight attendant gave her spiel—exits to the left, right, front and back, don't go to the lavatory because you'll disturb the beverage cart; try not to toss your cookies because no one wants to sit next to you, be quiet during the movie, and please do not ring the service bell because we are tired from our last flight. The usual. After they finished we were on our own for a while. Long enough for me to start the murder mystery packed in my carry-on, munch on a few Triscuits to ward off any airsickness, and wait for my Dramamine to kick in. Sure enough, in thirty minutes I drifted off to sleep but then jerked awake to pull out my neck pillow and blow it up, just in time to catch my nodding head, just in time to cradle my memories as I drifted off again.

I dreamt of that first phone call—the day of our first contact. The day I first spoke to my brother and my sister will be forever etched in my memory. Being awakened, startled and worried because of the early hour, confused by the accent of a stranger on the phone, shock and disbelief at the source of the call, and then, shivering in the early morning chill, not daring to ask them to hold while I got a robe or a blanket because the connection was so tenuous.

Later that day I met with a group of women for lunch. Before the food was served everyone went around the table to catch up on each others' happenings since last we met. My turn came last. I could hardly believe my own words as I said them out loud. I related my phone conversation with my brother. *Was I really using the word "brother?" The word "sister?"* When I finished talking, everyone had tears in their eyes and several said they had goosebumps while I told my story. I did too, for that matter. All those years I thought of myself as an only child. *What did the future hold?* I didn't know then that it would be many months before we would finally meet in person. Not until Labor Day weekend and this flight to Germany.

As the flight attendant brought dinner, I thought back to the first pictures I had seen of Dieter and his family. They had sent them by the Internet and I was so computer illiterate that I could barely figure out how to download them. It was so exciting to look for similarities. My niece had told me in our first conversation that I looked like her, and I could see it right away. I didn't really notice my similarities to my brother until I met him. I was flying to meet these people and *stay* with them. Me, who thinks that anything less than a four-star hotel is roughing it, was going to stay in a two-bedroom *one*-bathroom walkup apartment with three people I had never met. I was going to be in a foreign country, in a strange city—alone. However, had I not gone alone, I would never have had the spectacular experience I ended up having, living with my brother and his family, meeting my other siblings, spending every day together, staying up until the wee hours every night talking, translating, laughing, and eating chocolates.

While we ate our in-flight dinner, the man in the middle seat told me what he had paid for his ticket for the flight. It was less than half of what I paid, which was $1200.00. I did not do any price shopping for this trip. My brother didn't know about Labor Day and the inflated prices to fly on a holiday; he just knew he would have a week off from work and could spend time with me. I bought my ticket in June. That was the price, so I paid it. After all, I was going on the most important trip I would ever take. Who cared how much it cost?

Soon the flight was coming to an end. Before the plane landed, I went to the cracker box of a bathroom and spruced up. I had my travel toothpaste, my half-sized deodorant, a tiny cologne bottle, a comb, and a can of hairspray (yes, we could carry things like that on the plane back then). I changed my shoes and tried to look awake. Not an easy task. I was going to be meeting my family in a few minutes. I hoped I'd make at least a semi-good impression.

We landed at Schoenfeld Airport. Once off the plane, I felt like time was running out. I could hardly catch my breath and began to panic as I went through customs and then to get my luggage (several small bags that I hoped could be carried easily up to the second floor in a building with no elevator). Off came my first two bags, but not the third. As I stood and waited, I looked around me.

And there, through the glass was my whole family waiting for me, waving, laughing, blowing kisses. They weren't hard to miss. They were totally focused on me and their arms were loaded with flowers. And there I was, in what was the rather awkward position of just waiting and waiting and waiting for that third bag. Every few minutes I would turn, wave, and shrug my shoulders and point to the conveyer belt and hold up three fingers. Finally, my last bag came. I loaded it on the wheeled luggage carrier and pushed it through the door to the waiting area and my brothers Dieter, Klaus, Detti, my sister Helga, and my niece Ramona.

I remember I told myself to hold my head up high, keep my shoulders straight, and smile. I wanted to look bold, courageous, and confident. Never had I felt less so. I told myself, if you can teach ninety college students in a lecture hall, you can walk across the airport floor to your family and embrace them.

In a few short steps, I was in tears. I think my mind and body separated for a while. I now know what someone means when they say they had an out-of-body experience. I was seeing myself from above because I could not comprehend the experience I was having at the moment.

First my sister, Helga, shorter than I by five inches, stepped forward to hug me. We stared into each other's faces to see if we recognized any parts of ourselves in each other. I could not see any resemblance, at least not in her face. Later I would find many similarities in our taste in clothes, hair colors, and jewelry choices and believe me—neither of us had good taste in our younger years.

Next I hugged my brother, Klaus. He was taller than I was by an inch or two and very, very heavy; he had a big fat German tummy. He handed me his flowers, which I added to Helga's offering, and we hugged and kissed. This was my brother, but I did not see many similarities in our faces. Later I would come to find out we were both clowns, cut-ups, doing silly antics to get attention.

Then I turned and said, "You must be Detti? I'm so happy you could come to meet me." We hugged and kissed. More flowers. Detti was the tallest of the five of us. He and I definitely did not look alike. Later we discovered that we both collected elephants all our adult lives. Besides being tall, he was overweight, but not as heavy as Klaus. He stood supported with a bright purple crutch. My brother Dieter told me Detti was in poor health and he looked it. I remember being slightly afraid of him. He seemed much disheveled and reminded me of what I imagined a skid-row bum might look like.

Finally, I hugged and kissed my brother Dieter. I felt more familiar with him. This was the brother who spoke some English; this was the brother who had shared the most information with me. He was shorter than I was, but taller than Helga. He looked much younger than his 61 years. In his face I could see me: my eyes, my smile, my chin, and my relatively unlined face. During my stay, we discovered that we were like two peas in a pod or, as they say in Germany, "Like two left slippers."

And then finally I hugged the one that I felt the closest to at that time—my niece, Ramona. She was the person I had had the most contact with over the previous four months. She was my lifeline as everyone around me babbled in German. *What would this trip be like? How would we all communicate? This was only the first hour.*

They decided we would all go into the airport bar to chat. Helga, Dieter, Ramona, and Detti needed cigarettes. Detti and Helga needed a beer. Klaus and I sat at the other end of the table, away from the smokers, both of us being ex-smokers. I know the others were being considerate because I had previously shared that I had asthma and was a little concerned about the amount of smoking that would be taking place around me, although I did have my inhaler close at hand. We all looked each other over as they sat and talked quietly. Klaus tried to speak to me in halting English. My mind was running separately from my conversation. *What did they think of me? I found out later they thought I had the same looks and shape as my mother. Oh well, good to know that fat was in my genes and therefore not my fault.*

About an hour later Dieter stood up. We were going somewhere. I discovered that Helga and Klaus were returning to Helga's apartment. They would take the bus. Klaus had taken the train from Frankfurt to Berlin. I'm sure having a house guest for so long got old quickly. He arrived two weeks prior to my visit, was there for two weeks during my visit, and I was told he stayed another week after I left. Apparently, no one missed him at home. Probably his "wife," Irene, was glad to have their small apartment to herself.

Poor Helga. I discovered later that she had a one-bedroom flat and she let Klaus have her bedroom. She slept in a sleeping bag on the floor in the kitchen. Don't ask me why she didn't sleep on one of the many couches scattered around her large living room.

Detti took the bus back to his apartment. I didn't know then that I would only see him once again during my trip. Ramona, Dieter and I got into his car, an older Mercedes that he was very proud of, and we drove to their apartment to start the two-week search for my roots. *As I closed the door of the car I thought, "How lucky that all five of us are still alive."*

Chapter Twenty-Three

On The Other Side Of The Atlantic

I started my two-week journey without a map, a guide, or a clue what was happening from minute-to-minute. If you know me at all, that is *way* out of my comfort zone. I like to know what is happening days in advance, weeks in advance, years in advance; the uncertainty was difficult.

We hugged and kissed and waved goodbye to each other at the airport. I didn't know what was happening next, but I hoped it involved me going to bed for a while. We got the luggage into Dieter's small Mercedes. I rode in front with him while Ramona sat in the back. She spoke English very well, and I was so relieved about that. Dieter tried to tell me about points of interest along the way, but most of what he said I didn't understand. He had learned English at his job as a ground air traffic person who guided the planes into their proper spots after they landed. He had worked for Aeroflot in East Berlin before the wall came down, and Lufthansa hired him after that. He told me he lost all his accumulated pension when East Berlin was disassembled. As we drove through the streets I was rather shocked to see a billboard showing a naked man. Neither Dieter nor my niece seemed the least bit embarrassed by it, but Dieter did say, "You don't see those signs in America, do you?"

"No," I said.

Dieter, who had a lead foot, slowed to about 20 mph as we got closer to their apartment. He told me he had been *flashed* there a month before. My mind immediately conjured up an image of a little old man in a trench coat, bare legs, and black socks. I knowingly told him that, "Yes, that happens in American also." It was several days later that I found out that *flashing* in Germany meant getting caught by an automatic police camera that flashed as it took a picture of your car license if you tripped the speed trap. It wasn't until the end of my stay that I knew better, and we finally had a good laugh over my misconception.

We entered an industrial area where many of the apartments had balconies. Flowers were profuse in the window boxes and everywhere there were patches of green space. The Paul (my family's last name was Paul) family apartment was old but well maintained. Across the street from them was a military hospital, and next door was a huge government building. There were no corner cafes or flower shops or markets in this area. It was a quiet neighborhood of apartments and offices. Behind their apartment building was a park-like area about two blocks long and one block wide. It had lots of benches and lovely old trees.

They were able to keep their cars in the alleyway between the green space and their apartment building. Dieter and his wife Eszter each owned a car, which was quite extravagant in Berlin, but they both worked and needed them. Neither my brother Detti nor my sister had ever owned a car. Perhaps Klaus had one for transporting people in his job, but I don't know for sure. Berlin has an excellent mass transit system. Students rode it for free, so Ramona, a college student, saved lots of money on transportation. Also in the green space by the apartment was an enormous clothesline. Every tenant was allowed three lines for their clothes. My sister-in-law had a tiny washing machine—in her kitchen—but no dryer. Clothes were hung outside. When it rained the clothes just stayed on the line longer. Because I could not be parted from my limited wardrobe for too long, I washed my unmentionables in the bathroom sink and dried them on Ramona's step machine in her room—*my* room for the duration.

Not one of my siblings lived in an apartment with an elevator. Turned out it was only one-and-a-half flights up to Dieter's apartment, which suited me just fine. Before we even got to the top, Eszter, my fiery, Hungarian sister-in-law, was there to greet me. She hugged me and laughed and was the warmest, friendliest person you could ever meet. I was delighted with her. She spoke not a word of English and was teased by her husband and daughter because she didn't speak German all that well, either. She and Dieter met when he was allowed, by Russian officials, to vacation in Hungary—another Iron Curtain country. They fell in love and eventually learned each other's languages, married, and he moved her to East Berlin.

After greeting me, she hurried into the tiny kitchen to finish preparations for a wonderful breakfast. It smelled divine—dark bread, cheeses, butter, meats. Breakfast was scrumptious and I learned over time that Eszter was a fantastic cook.

I told them I *had* to lie down for a while and to wake me in three hours. Dieter showed me how to work the toilet in the bathroom (seems all German toilets work differently from each other and from our American "standardized" toilets). Then he showed me how the "occupied" signal worked that he had designed. When I entered the lockless bathroom, I was to flip a switch and the light would go on outside the door. Then people would know the bathroom was busy. We actually managed—the four of us—with one bathroom. Back home Jim and Ann and I had three bathrooms for three people.

As I lay on the bed, almost sick to my stomach with fatigue, my mind refused to turn off. I thought back to the morning's encounter. The hugging, the tears, the feeling of floating out of my body. At first, I wasn't totally sure who was Detti and which one was Klaus, because most of the photos they sent were when they were all much younger. Even in that short time, I realized that Dieter was the leader of the group. I learned over time he was the glue that held the family together.

I hugged three brothers and my sister that morning. My sister held me very tight, much moved by my presence. Klaus had a huge, beaming smile, his delight in being there and meeting me very obvious. Detti and Helga were close, and she had told him he had to be at the airport to greet me. Klaus was the typical rotund, jolly German. He was happy to have a sister that was a, as he kept saying, "rich American professor." I tried to dissuade him from that belief, but I don't think I managed. In Germany, people who taught at the university level were well paid and held in high esteem. He assumed, incorrectly, that it was the same at the universities and colleges in America.

What would people in that airport that day think if they knew what they were witnessing? How could they know what an unusual "family" they were walking past? How is it possible that no one took a photo? I think we were all being respectful of a moment that could only be experienced once and never again—that *first* moment? I wonder if we had met for the first time now, years later, with all of us having cell phones that we might not have started immortalizing the day by snapping away. At that time residents of Germany had "handys" (cell phones) but in America it was not so common. Jim and I had a mobile phone, but it was huge and we used it in the car for road trips.

Eszter was a joy. I loved her immediately. Despite our language barrier, we communicated perfectly throughout the trip. She would jabber at me in her combination German/Hungarian. Her expressive eyes and face and constant hand gestures helped me understand her. I did the same, using my limited traveler's German to make myself understood. She must have remembered what it was like to come to Germany and meet her new family and have limited communication skills because she was so empathetic toward me. She would tell me ways that she thought I was like my mother. She told me my fingers and fingernails were like my mother's. *What an odd thing to find out.*

My husband, Jim, sent an email to Dieter and Ramona after he dropped me off at the airport in La Crosse. I didn't know he was going to attempt to write it in German. He used my dictionary to compose it. *"Guten Abend. Bonnie ist auf Sie fahrt zu Berlin. Ich gerecht zuruckkehen von der Flughafen. Auf Wiedersehen. Onkel, Jim."*

I sent my first email to Jim from my brother's house. The German keyboard had some letters and symbols in entirely different places. It took too long to figure it out, so I decided I would just type as if it was my keyboard at home and hope that Ann and Jim could figure it out.

"Hi. I'm here. The flights were all good. Everzthing on time. Thez were all waiting for me and I could see them, but I had to pick up my suitcases first and then go through customs. Even Detti came and it was wonderful to hug everzone. And lots of tears, too, but happy ones. We have had a wonderful German breakfast that Eszter made and now I'm going to take a nap. Don#t know what we are going to do later. I am to tzpe off line and then Ramona will turn on the computer and send it. Thez loved zour e-mail. Thez have laughed a lot about zour German—zou made a great trz. I love zou."

Jim and I wrote back and forth to each other over the course of the next two weeks. At first, I was dazed and in awe of what was happening around me, but later, as I started to get my bearings, I used the computer to keep a diary of what was happening each day. I would write to Jim (and Ann) and fill them in on what we did each day. I did a little *editing* of my perceptions because I knew that my niece could read each of my emails before they were sent.

I told Jim about going into the café at the airport after we collected my luggage and sat at separate ends of the table—the smokers vs. the non-smokers. "It was so special to be with them all." I told him how on the way to Dieter's apartment, I drank in the neighborhood sites. I saw Berlin in a different light—this was my birthplace. I might have grown up here had fate not intervened.

Ramona's room was tiny by American standards. It was long and narrow with very high ceilings; narrow enough that you could touch both sides of the room if you stretched out your arms. She slept on a futon, which was quite comfortable. I was to occupy her room for the next two weeks. The futon had silk sheets. I think they thought I would love that, but I didn't. It was impossible to stay in one place in the bed and my pillow kept sliding onto the floor. I felt that I would slide right off the bed, too. When her futon was open there was barely enough room to slip out of bed or to open the door.

Besides Ramona's bedroom, bathroom, and kitchen (the three long, narrow rooms) there was a large, square living room with twenty-foot high ceilings, and a master bedroom. All the windows were very tall, and Eszter had gorgeous Hungarian lace hanging on them as curtains. Dieter had built floor-to-ceiling cupboards along one wall of the living room for storage.

After my first nap, we had a great lunch. Then I needed another nap. I forced myself to only sleep for one and a half hours before we had afternoon tea, which usually happened about 5 p.m. It's a huge part of being German. This day it was cream puffs and *apfelkuchen mit cream*. Then Dieter and I took a stroll (he liked *strolling*, not *walking*, and never briskly) in the neighborhood. I couldn't believe I was walking down the streets of my birthplace WITH MY BROTHER!

It was heartbreaking to discover that in all the years they lived in this apartment they were only *one block* from the Wall. It was what Ramona looked at until 1989. The Wall.

They were only a few blocks from the River Spree and there was a walking path that wandered along the river and through the old cemetery. After the war, the Russians had built the Wall right over the gravestones. Parts of the Wall had been left standing so people would remember. We passed by an old watchtower, no longer armed with guards, but still a reminder of how horrible those times were. Later that evening, Dieter Gave me two pieces of the Wall he had saved as souvenirs, and now was sharing with me. He told me how he hated the Russians and of ways he tried to sabotage them whenever he could. It was an incredible walk through history—one that they lived and lived *through*, and one that I had avoided. *I wondered: Was it better to be adopted and raised in America or better to live under Russian occupation, but be with my family?*

By the time that walk was over I felt like I had known Dieter my whole life. Our conversation was easy and comfortable despite a few language problems. Neither of us felt hampered. We just tried to find a different way to express ourselves; hand gestures, facial expressions, or just different words.

Back in the apartment, Dieter showed me a home movie of my mother—our mother. It was taken when Ramona was a baby and shortly before Mama, as they called her, died. I drank in the sight of my very own mother. It was such a brief glimpse. She had my body (sigh) and thick glasses because she had cataracts, but she was smiling and happy.

After the video I felt almost ill from lack of sleep so I had to lie down again…for an hour. When I got up we had supper at 8 p.m. We grilled our own choices of meat (a huge variety) on a hibachi grill set up on the coffee table in the living room in front of the couch; it was their dining room table. That's the way they ate when company was there. That was fine, but after many meals leaning over to reach my plate, I experienced some gastrointestinal issues. Dinner that night was fun and filling. I was feeling better about one thing I had worried about—food. I had brought along several boxes of granola bars in case I didn't like Eszter's cooking, but she was a splendid cook. Later I brought out all the bars (enough for two meals a day for two weeks) and gave them to Ramona. She became a chewy bar fan forever.

Chapter Twenty-Four

Digging Into The Past

The next day I was up at 8:30. We had another wonderful breakfast of bits and pieces—cheeses, meats, eggs, crackers, and other "delicacies" I didn't want to look at or taste. Dieter still had some days he had to work at the airport, but on the days that he was not working we would drive around Berlin and he would show me where I *would have gone* to grade school, where I *would have been* baptized, the hospital I was born in, where I *would have lived* if I had not been given away, which was an old, white apartment building. In between all the sightseeing, we spent a lot of time at the government offices and at the copy center. We were in search of my official, legal, original birth certificate.

Dieter would drive around the block three times trying to find a close parking spot. I told him I could certainly walk a few blocks, but that's not the German way. When we would meet with someone in charge of documents who might give us some answers, I would sit quietly and listen to Dieter and the government person speaking to each other at lightning speed. The official would usually steal curious glances at me, but my mind would drift, thinking of the beginning. *How far I'd come, how unique my circumstances were, how lucky I was to have finally found my family.*

Before I arrived, Dieter had done as much legwork as he could manage. Some of the papers he found shocked him to the core. One such document showed that our birth parents, Erika and Gerhard were *remarried* on June 4, 1948 only a little over a month before I was born. None of my siblings even knew they had been divorced (1946) much less remarried. Dieter didn't know what to make of this new revelation. He said they must have remarried because she was pregnant with me. Later Klaus and Helga said they remembered that Mama was pregnant in 1948, but she did not come home from the hospital with a baby. In those days children didn't ask questions of their parents and certainly nothing that intimate. She went to her grave never telling any of my siblings that they had a younger sister.

After my birth mother, Erika, died, Dieter the self-appointed historian was going through the family bible and noticed that there was paperwork showing the birth of two children—one named Rainer in 1945 and another named Gerda Erika in 1948. There were no accompanying death certificates. When he went to the records office to get the official documents of death, he was given a copy of Rainer's death certificate. He had died at only a few months old and would have been about three years older than I was. However, Dieter found that Gerda (me) did not die as he had assumed, but had been adopted. He did his best to trace me, at least for the first four years of my life. This search, unbelievably, led him back to the same apartment building where he and his whole family lived in 1948. *Did we all live in this crumbling, decrepit apartment building at the same time?*

We know that my alleged birth father, Gerhard, wrote a letter agreeing to give me up for adoption in 1950, but I was born in 1948 and baptized in September of that year with Dorothy's last name. Nothing legal about a baptismal certificate, however. *Why in the world did it take two years for my birth father to write that paper? Were my birth parents and my first adoptive mother in contact? Why was my address listed as being the same building in which he and the rest of the family resided?* Dieter hoped that the Red Cross could help him find me, but the trail ran cold in 1952. Of course, that is when Dorothy brought me to American.

The first afternoon I was in Berlin, Dieter took me to the cemetery. My mother, her husband (I didn't know then who Gerhard was to me), and my maternal grandmother, Anna, were all in a plot together with their names on a single headstone. Dieter had to pay yearly to keep them in the front part of the cemetery, otherwise, after a prescribed number of years (20 I believe), graves were moved to the back of the cemetery and only a numbered plaque would mark where they were. Dieter is very sentimental, and he didn't want them dug up and relegated to the back. The cemetery was beautiful; full of fresh bouquets. If you wished you could plant rose bushes that were sold at the entrance. The owners of the cemetery let you borrow a shovel and dig a hole anywhere on your plot. I bought a sweetheart rose bush and Dieter planted it for me. I did cry a little and Dieter walked away and left me on my own for a bit. Then he started taking pictures of me. Like me, he's the official photographer in the family and he was taking pictures all the time.

I steeled myself for a feeling of overwhelming grief as I stood at my mother's grave. However, that feeling did not come. All I felt was sadness that I had never known her. No matter how hard I tried to feel bad about having been raised apart from my siblings, I had to temper that feeling with knowing that they were raised in poverty, behind the Iron Curtain, while I was raised with privilege in a free country.

One thing threw me for a loop as I stood gazing at the headstone. I was reading the dates on the stone marker and discovered something surprising. My father (known to me only at this time as the husband of my mother) and my grandmother both died in 1977. Jim and I had a baby who died (on the day he was born) in 1977. An old wives' tale is that death "comes in threes" - it wasn't until 23 years later that I discovered it was true. Unfortunately, I was unable to find the right words to express this to Dieter at the moment, and so I kept it to myself. Later I explained it to Ramona and she was able to translate it to Dieter.

We then drove to another cemetery—this one overgrown and weedy—where Gerhard's parents were buried. I didn't have a lot of interest then, as I was positive he was not my father.

My birth grandmother, my birth father, and my birth mother's gravestone. Notice Anna and Gerhard both died in 1977.

Chapter Twenty-Five

Getting to Know All About You

The next day Dieter took me to Helga's apartment. I was worried about walking up four flights of stairs because of my asthma. When we arrived on the street below her apartment we heard someone yelling. Looking up, I saw Helga hanging out over the windowsill. She was so excited I was coming to her apartment. I huffed and puffed and arrived slightly sweaty at her door. She was welcoming and very effusive (*probably a few sips of Schnapps before we arrived*). Klaus was there also, and once I got to know him better I realized he was already probably getting on Helga's nerves. She did a lot of eye-rolling behind his back while he spoke. When we walked through the door, Klaus started to show me her apartment as if it was his. Helga cursed him in German and took over.

Helga had no intention of learning English and had told Dieter, "Let her (meaning me) learn German, she is younger." He said she liked being in control, but also he was sure she just didn't want to miss any of the conversation. She ruled the roost, that was for sure. Consequently, because she forbade any English to be spoken when she was in the room, I missed out on a lot of the conversation.

I was there for only ten minutes when the phone rang. Helga answered and handed the phone to me. I could not figure out who would be calling me except Jim. However, it was Helga's best friend, Gisela, calling to welcome me to Berlin. She spoke perfect English without any accent. She had lived in America during part of her marriage. It was nice to speak to her, but very distracting. I wanted to be part of the conversation with my family and I didn't want to talk to this stranger.

I could see my siblings sizing me up again. Dieter was constantly videotaping me, and it made my conversation with Gisela stilted. I wish I could have talked to her privately and asked her questions about Helga. In the months and years following my first visit, Helga would call me when Gisela and she were together so I could talk with Gisela and we could get her to do some translating. However, Gisela was very loyal to Helga and never revealed anything personal about her good friend.

Soon my phone call to Gisela was finished and we had tea and coffee cake, followed by all of them giving me gifts. I got a 10 X 12 wax picture from Klaus that he claimed was 100 years old. He said it was not from our family but from the family of his son's wife. He told me he gave up two of his three sons for adoption and that one was in America. He said Irene was his common-law wife and I found out from Dieter that Klaus had a wife, Ermgard, and two daughters, Gabbi born in 1956 and Getti born in 1959 from a marriage when he was 18 years old. They never divorced because she was Catholic. In about 1994 Irene felt bad about having given up her two younger sons and searched for them. Apparently, it was Irene's father who forced her to give up her babies back when they were born.

She found one son, Gerald, living in Utah and one son, Dieter, who had been raised in an orphanage in Germany, but Klaus and Irene had never been to visit them. As he showed me photos he had brought with him to Berlin, I saw the clown in him—the silly expressions, the silly outfits. I do that too—make silly faces when I'm being photographed. He pulled out his harmonica and played *My Bonnie Lies over the Ocean*. Later I found out that Mama knew where Klaus was after he ran away to Frankfurt and had even managed to visit him. She had not told Gerhard or the other kids. At first, anyway. *Apparently, she was good at keeping all kinds of secrets.*

Helga enjoyed showing me her apartment. It was large, old, and full of the mementos that people find on travels and throughout life. It reminded me of me, always having collections of things. I discovered we both collected turtles just as later I discovered that Detti and I both collected elephants.

Helga was the oldest—calm, quiet, and sometimes gazing away like she was not paying attention. She didn't seem to care if she made a good impression. Dieter shared with me that she had fought bladder cancer more than once. I would have thought it more likely that it would be lung cancer because of how much she smoked, and only years later did I find out that bladder cancer is a very common cancer from smoking.

Her apartment reeked of smoke, but in deference to me, she went onto her balcony to smoke while I visited. She smoked four packs a day. I used to smoke one pack a day and knew how bad that was. I don't think she liked going outside to smoke, but Dieter told her she had to. At that time, Dieter, Ramona, and Detti also smoked. Klaus had quit, and so had I. Smoking seemed to be the national pastime in Germany. No non-smoking signs and no non-smoking sections in restaurants. Like it or leave it.

Over time I found out bits and pieces about Gerhard, my mother's husband. He was a soldier and he ran his house in a military fashion. All the children slept in one room. In the morning he would go in and blow a whistle, whereupon they would have to jump out of bed and stand at attention. They would have to do 75 pushups and 100 deep knee bends, or so Klaus and Dieter agreed. (Having my adoptive dad come in and pull the covers off me after the third call didn't seem so bad in hindsight.) When they cleaned their room, he would come in with a white glove and inspect it. Klaus ran away because Gerhard beat him with a tennis racket. He used it on all of them except Helga, but on Klaus the most. Once they overheard him threaten to hit Erika and she told him that she would hit him on the head with a frying pan. *Yea, Mama.*

That first day at Helga's ended with coffee cake and other sweet goodies, which is always the afternoon staple. I started to worry I might gain twenty pounds by the end of the two weeks. At 7 p.m. we left. I had learned so much. When we got back to Dieter's, Eszter had dinner waiting for us. I got the impression that the two women—Eszter and Helga—didn't get along too well. No wonder. Eszter was sweet and easy going, Helga was stern and bossy. Being with Eszter made me calm; made me feel wanted and loved. Secretly I wished she were my sister. Helga was overbearing and kind of scary. She seemed impatient and domineering.

Dinner was fried zucchini and meatballs served with the ever-present cucumber, tomato, radish, and pepper mixture. Little wieners and sausages seemed to be a mainstay. Everything was fried; Eszter had a large deep fryer on the kitchen counter. Breakfast the next day was five-minute eggs. Dieter and I put them in little egg cups and cracked them. After dinner that night all four of us sat and talked forever. I tried to speak as much German as I could for Eszter's sake. Ramona did a lot of translating, which was very tiring for her. Dieter had to get up at 3 a.m. for work so he finally went to bed. The next day I would be spending the day with Helga. *Not a happy prospect in my mind.*

Ramona would take me there and Dieter would pick me up at 3:30 p.m. I pictured a long day of Helga not letting Klaus or me speak English. Luckily Klaus spoke half-German and half-English despite her edict. I felt that at least he was willing to "protect" me.

Helga spent a lot of time on her balcony smoking cigarettes and often would go in her kitchen to have swigs of beer. A balcony is a treasured commodity in Berlin; it makes an apartment seem bigger and allows people to feel like they are outside.

And so that day ended. Loving it. Hating it. Running the emotional gamut and homesick for Jim; heartsick that it had taken me so long to find my family and just plain sick from eating all the fried foods.

The only time the five of us were ever together other than at the airport when I arrived. Helga, Klaus, Dieter, Gerda (me), and Detti.

Chapter Twenty-Six

Bridging the Past and the Present

"*Was ist unrecht mit mein* German?" Jim continued to amuse my family with his attempts at writing German. My brother and niece got a big kick out of it. Jim wrote in English about things at home. I loved to hear from him, but that world was so far away. What I was experiencing was mindboggling and all-consuming.

I knew I had to return to my real world in Wisconsin soon. I knew that I had to get back to teaching my classes at the university and that laundry and cooking and grocery shopping would become my daily life again. At the moment, though, on day three of my visit, I was immersed in a world of discovery. *Who was I? Who were these people who had become my siblings? How were we alike? It was easier to see how we were different; there were so many differences. Lives lived in such different manners, different cities, different goals, expectations, and desires; different people guiding us, shaping us, influencing us.*

This morning was similar to the day before. Dieter and Eszter went to work. Ramona and I slept in a little and I had my favorite breakfast of hard rolls, cheese, and meat. Then Ramona took me to Helga's and this time she stayed with me, thank God. Ramona and Helga seemed to have some kind of a love/hate relationship. The conversations between them were heated, like WWIII was breaking out. Klaus, the clown, was his usual hospitable self, always ready to entertain and keep the conversation going. Oddly, we both carried our own teabags around with us.

Helga got out a box of photos. She sat on my left and Klaus on my right while Ramona sat in the kitchen and did some homework. Helga would take out a photo, look at it, hand it to me and point to a person in the photo and say, "Helga." I would look and then pass it on to Klaus. In many of the photos, I saw that she and I had the same garish taste in clothes. She loved loud, colorful outfits and I did too (*that was before I evolved into the classy, sophisticated clothes maven that I am today*).

A number of pictures were of Anna, my grandmother, and I was struck by how much some of them looked like our daughter, Ann. Then, out of the blue came two pictures in a row of Helga —naked—standing in front of the TV in her apartment. I was shocked to say the least. She looked about 35 in the photos. Again, she punched the picture and said, "Helga," and I passed it on to Klaus. When she saw what I had done she snatched it out of his hand. What did I know? I thought maybe if it was acceptable to show your new sister naked photos of yourself it was okay to show them to your brother, too. Later I discovered that Dieter, Eszter, and Ramona had gone to a nudist camp on several occasions, although Ramona assured me that she and her mother did not take off all their clothes. Different culture. Different world. Different standards.

Lunch was potato soup. Picture adding warm water to German potato salad. Helga put a wiener in the bottom of the soup bowl. We only had a soup spoon to eat with, but I discovered that we were supposed to fish the wiener out with our fingers.

Helga's bathroom was like Dieter's, which meant about a foot wider than the bathtub. She, like Dieter, kept the window open at all times, and that meant it was very cold in the bathroom. It's their version of an air-freshener. Everyone complained about the cold, but no one closed that window. I had to close it when I took my shower in the morning or I would not have had enough soap to cover all the goosebumps on my body. I would open it again when I was dressed. Helga also had a washing machine in her kitchen that she was very proud of. No one did any ironing. That was okay because no one got very dressed up.

I wondered at the simplicity of the German lifestyle. They were happy in an apartment with no elevator. They were happy with a clothes washer even though there was no dryer. They were happy with a tiny refrigerator although it meant going to the store many times a week. They were happy with less. They didn't need to own their living spaces; they were happy to have a car—or not. They expected less and were not disappointed with what they had.

Owning a tiny "garden house" was the best thing that could happen to a city dweller. Helga had a garden house a block from her apartment and she took Klaus and me to see it. The building itself was the size of a one-car garage. It had a fenced-in garden plot in front of it, also the size of a one-car garage. It had a cot and an electric cooler and not much else, but she would spend nights there when it was too hot in her unairconditioned apartment.

She had very bad feet and, according to Dieter, she did not go too many places anymore because of the tremendous amount of steps. Her garden was quite neglected. She had a storage unit in the basement of her building and she would call Dieter on the phone and tell him to come over and bring up a case of beer from the unit and carry it up to her apartment for her—four and a half flights. Then he was expected to keep the beer replenished in the storage area.

Klaus goofed around in the garden, just as he did everywhere. I found out he was very afraid of bees. He made me laugh, and I felt comfortable with him. He was missing his two bottom teeth, which made him even sillier at times. He sang any songs that came into his head, which is something I do, too. He loved gadgets and was fascinated by my German electronic translation machine (about the size of a pack of cigarettes) that I brought over with me.

It was a great little device because it would translate not only words but whole phrases that were typed into it. Dieter and I used it quite a bit, but it was Klaus who *desired* it. I could see he was angling for me to buy him one, but they were not cheap and I had already bought and sent over many gifts for each of them. Quite a costly enterprise considering four siblings and my niece and my sister-in-law to buy for.

I brought along some jewelry I thought I might give to my family depending on how I felt and if they looked like they would like jewelry. I ended up giving Eszter and Ramona several rings and bracelets. Klaus complimented my white tennis shoes—not a big ticket item in Germany. I guess they made me stand out as an American. My feet were comfortable so I didn't care. He gave me his shoe size and asked me to send him a pair. I said I would, but I never remembered to do so.

Klaus had been a courier of some sort in Frankfurt. He did this for many years. He also tried his hand at many different things to earn money but never kept a job very long. Dieter said that Klaus was lazy and that was why Gerhard (our father) was harder on him than the others. Dieter confirmed that Gerhard beat the boys, especially Klaus, and badly enough that Klaus could not go to school some days because of the marks. *Did I have my answer yet? Was it better to be raised by Gerhard, always toeing the line and living in abject poverty, but with my siblings?*

Detti was another interesting personality. His first wife Johanna gave him two sons. With his second wife, he had a daughter and with his third wife another daughter. With his fourth wife, a son who now lives in Munich. He was a very successful house painter, but with each divorce, he left with his suitcase in hand and lost his house and his money. By the time I met him he had no money and was living off the state and drinking excessively.

He lived in the apartment of a much older woman. Dieter said she was his "sugar mama." The reason that he and Dieter had a falling-out was that Detti was always getting drunk and ordering Dieter to drive him somewhere. Dieter got sick and tired of doing it and one day just refused to do it. Detti didn't talk to him for years. Until the day I showed up at the airport.

I learned that my mother was a saver and also that she was not much of a drinker, didn't like to work, and didn't like getting up early. *So, I come by* that *naturally.* She loved to party, dance, and socialize. *The apple does not fall far from the tree.* The only job she ever had was running a bed and breakfast for a few years during the war, when her husband was a prisoner of war in France, to make ends meet. Klaus said she made and sold bread and jams during the war.

Dieter said that Erika's father and uncle were very tall. I'm taller than Helga and Dieter, but shorter than Klaus and Detti. Mama had straight hair. It was her husband, Gerhard, who had the curly hair—like my curly hair—but that was just a coincidence in my mind.

Mama and Dieter were quite vociferous about hating the Communists. As a lark, Helga apparently joined the Communist Party when she was 16 but stopped quickly. Gerhard would warn the family to be careful when criticizing the Communists because a person could be thrown in jail for such things. Dieter said that one time someone put a Communist flag in the front lawn and Mama went out after dark, broke it in two, and threw it on the ground. When Dieter was teaching mechanics at the airlines he was approached by his boss and told that he could not say bad things about the Communists anymore or he would have to quit teaching. Dieter quit right then and there and gave up the extra pay because he said he would not be told that he could not say what he liked.

In 2000, at the time of my visit, Dieter was the oldest employee at Lufthansa. He had been a ground control person and all communication with the pilots had to be in the international language of English. He also knew Russian and later Hungarian. Gerhard knew French, probably because of his time as a prisoner of war in France. Dieter no longer worked on the planes or guided them in. By 2000 he was allowed to sit on a chair and check luggage.

Years before the airlines job, he worked in air conditioning during the day and played in a band at night. He was playing in his band the night the Berlin Wall went up. He said that people ran into the bar around two in the morning and yelled that the Russians were setting up a row of tall concrete barriers all around town. Dieter said he didn't really believe them at first.

In three days, the Russians enclosed the Russian sector of Berlin and it became "East Berlin." Then over the next few months they built a second wall several yards from the first and topped it with barbed wire and installed guard houses with armed guards. I asked Dieter why they didn't flee before that point and he said, "Where would we go? And how could we know if it would be better?"

After three days it was too late. All the holes had been plugged, but thousands had escaped during that time. After that, someone from East Berlin could never ask permission to join their family in West Berlin because if they did, suddenly they or a loved one would lose their job, or worse. In the 1980s there was some letup in the restrictions for vacations outside of East Berlin, but they still had to remain in the Eastern sector, and that is when Dieter met and fell in love with Eszter in Hungary. They married in October 1975.

Dieter said the East Germans liked Gorbachev because he promised he would withdraw the Russian troops. That gave them much hope. Once people turned 60 (women) and 65 (men) Russia had no use for them anymore, and they were free to leave. Mama and Gerhard would visit Helga in West Berlin and went to Frankfurt to see Klaus.

On my fourth day, Dieter and I went again to look for a copy of my original birth certificate. The big holdup was that neither my driver's license nor my passport had my birth name on it. I had brought along the form that stated that I had legally changed my name to Bonnie Ann from Mary Susan but there was nothing connecting *Gerda Erika Paul* with those other names. I called Jim and had him gather all the paperwork I had back home with my many names on them and had his sister scan and forward it all to Ramona.

That night, back at the apartment, Eszter made us chicken and potato salad, lettuce salad, and then a sweet treat. We sat and looked at more photos. I wrote to Jim.

"More and more I think that I'm Gerhard's daughter. The photos are such a giveaway. Only thing is, I can't tell them what I'm thinking until I get back to La Crosse and find the photos of me that look so much like him. We will never know why they gave me away, but we will do DNA testing and find out if we are half or whole siblings."

Sitting with my sister-in-law every night after
dinner – eating, chatting, and laughing.

Chapter Twenty-Seven

Day Four—Time Is Flying By

"Hope your research into your past goes well. *Geniessen Ihr zeit* in Germany. *Mein guten abend zu alle! Auf Wideresehen. Liebe,* Jim" And this is how Jim ended his email to me dated September 7, 2000. I wrote back, *"When I get home I expect a big breakfast set for me everz morning with a table cloth and manz meats and cheeses and breads and a five-minute soft boiled egg—schmect gut!"*

Dieter told me that our mother always said, *"Essen und trinken halt Leib und Seele zusammen* (eating and drinking hold body and soul together.) I found out my mother hated spicy food and sour food. *Me too.* She didn't smoke although she is holding a cigarette in her hand in photos a couple times. Later in the day Eszter and I walked to the post office to get some stamps for me, and then to the grocery store for more meats and cheeses.

I enjoyed the store. It was called Aldi. Although they opened Aldi in my hometown later, they didn't have them in Wisconsin then. I was amazed that you put a coin into the grocery cart to use it and when you return it you get the coin back. We passed a 13-million marks (7 million dollar) memorial to the Wall on our way home, but Eszter was not happy about the structure because she said it would have been better if the government had spent that money on the people instead.

Later that night Klaus appeared at Dieter's apartment unexpectedly. He never told Helga where he was. She was worried and called there. He complained about her and she complained about him, and poor Eszter just had to sit and listen and be sympathetic. His shirts were bursting at the buttons because his stomach was so big. He didn't care. He just laughed. He thought that I had a lot of money. He repeated, "You rich teacher. You teach at university."

I could not convince him that in the United States being a teacher is not a high-paying job and that I was only "ad hoc" and did not have a doctorate. He was sure I had enough money to buy him a motor home. Ramona became quite concerned that I would fall for his line, but I assured her that I could see him quite clearly for who and what he was—a hypochondriac and a free-loader, but a good-hearted person. And he was the only one of my siblings with my same color eyes—hazel. Erika's were brown and Gerhard's were blue.

The evening of September 9, 2000, I wrote an email to Jim about my day at the weekend house. I was so excited to tell Jim that Dieter, like me, never got bitten by mosquitoes. I also discovered that Dieter and Mama both loved piping hot soup and very hot tea, like I do. And neither Dieter nor I like our soup to be thick.

Papa Gerhard was the musical one in the family. Both he and Erika would go to the theatre or a concert once a month. It was forbidden to listen to American music in the East, but when the family would go to the beach along the Baltic Sea they would listen to transistor radios. That's how Dieter came to know and love '60^s music. He asked me, "What is a hound dog?" (From Elvis' song.) Dieter and Klaus and I sang in the car a lot.

On the way to the weekend house (which is about a 45-minute drive from their apartment) Klaus, Dieter, and I went to see Sanssoucci Palace. It was beautiful. Klaus had great difficulty breathing. It was rather alarming. The exertion of walking the grounds and his great girth were the reason, I suspect. Luckily, I did fine with the walking (I was worried about my plantar fasciitis).

That night Dieter made Hungarian goulash over an open fire pit. It was spicy (*not my favorite thing in the world*) and basically a clear liquid with vegetables in it. We all "tasted" it from the same serving spoon. I ate some because I was so hungry and wished I had brought my chewy bars to the weekend house instead of leaving them at the apartment. Luckily I did bring my coat and sweater. It got chilly at night in September.

Dieter saw me as the most special person in the world and was so happy I found them. He would grin and hug me whenever he looked at me. He said he always wanted to hug Helga, but she was cold and standoffish. He was thrilled he had a new sister he could hug, and that made him even more special to me. I noticed that his ears were shaped like mine and we had the same flat spot on the back of our heads.

We both loved sweet tea. We loved murder mysteries and hated scary movies. Whenever we took a walk, it was a stroll—and that was fine with me. (I could never keep up with Ann or Jim when we were walking. I take small steps, like my mother Mary taught me....ladylike at all times, of course.) And when we went to the grocery store, Dieter bought eggs and checked each egg in the carton to make sure it was not cracked. I do that all the time.

I told Dieter, Eszter, and Ramona about buying our land in Arizona and that we would be building on it soon. I didn't mention it to Helga or Klaus because I knew they would think we were rich. Owning two houses was so different from their apartment living. *Keep in mind: Germany is about the size of Wisconsin.*

Klaus talked once or twice about a son in Utah. I didn't realize he was referring to a son he had given up for adoption. Why would he have a son in Utah? Sometimes I didn't understand what he was trying to tell me about Erika or about his life. It was sad not to know exactly what happened to each of my siblings in their childhoods, young adulthoods, and throughout their lives. The language barrier was a true barrier in so many ways.

Klaus was what we in America would call a freeloader and I was disappointed that I had a brother who seemed like an opportunist, but I still came to love him. He would beg or cajole something out of anyone he could. I did give him money for the train trip he took to and from Berlin to meet me. No matter his personality, I was so happy to have met him.

Helga always carried three to four different brands of cigarettes with her. She chain-smoked and "chain-drank" beer. She smiled very little and seemed very distant. I guess it just was her personality. Maybe the war had affected her. She never had any children, although I did ask Ramona to ask Helga if it was possible that I was perhaps *her* child and that Erika just claimed me to save face. Helga laughed and emphatically said, "No!" *I thought maybe it might have been possible because Helga was sixteen when I was born.* One time she asked Ramona to ask me if my teeth were real because they were so perfect. *They were all real.* Helga's were all false.

We studied my birth certificate and my first adoption papers over and over while I was there. We couldn't figure out why everything was dated 1950 when I was born in 1948. We wondered if Dorothy (my second mother) didn't legally adopt me until 1950. And if so, why?

Jim wrote and said that he was not serving me a big German breakfast until I started my day with pushups and sit-ups like Gerhard made the other kids do. He then told me, "You can pick your friends and you can pick your nose, but you can't pick your relatives. That's all I'm going to say." *Ha. Thanks, Jim.* He ended with, "*Ich hoffen euer wochhe ende an der hause in land wunderbar.*" Ramona and Dieter got such a big kick out of Jim's attempts. *I think he was talking about us having a wonderful time at the weekend house.*

Back to the weekend house. It was small. It had a tiny bathroom, tiny kitchen, a living room with a pull out sofa, a TV, and a tiny bedroom. It had a large, roofed porch to keep off the rain with plenty of room for grilling on the patio with several tables to eat at outside. There was a peach tree. In German it's *Pfirsich,* and you are supposed to spit out the first letters to say it correctly. I tried and tried and just couldn't quite get it, and we all laughed until we had to hold our sides from the pain. There were also several apple trees that Eszter made applesauce and apple jelly from. Little is wasted in Germany.

All the other weekend houses had large gardens, each enclosed with a fence. And each fence had a different personality—the charming picket fence, the forbidding chain link fence, and some were just crossed logs. There were paths for everyone to walk to each other's property and their own. The paths were grass and about as wide as a car. There were 99 plots (each about 100' by 50') and they had been deeded to the airline employees in about 1985 – the drawback was they were directly under the flight paths of the planes.

Dieter and I walked around to see the other cottages and each time he saw someone he knew he introduced me as his "sister from America". Then they would start speaking to me in rapid German and Dieter would laugh and say I didn't speak German. They would look confused and he was delighted. They were all welcoming. One lady insisted we come in for tea and cookies. Another had many cats and I said I liked cats, so she had to introduce me to each of the twenty she could find. Another lady simply decided to join us on our stroll—a stroll into another time where people all knew each other and life was unhurried and simple. *I loved it. It is a memory I will always carry with me.*

I wrote and told Ann that Ramona was a lot like her. Ramona was always grumbling about the bicyclists or drivers and she talked to them as if they could hear her. Ramona was very impatient, also a trait that Ann possessed. And they both suffered from GERD. I found out that Ramona hated TV shows about hospitals and emergency rooms. She hated blood, just like her cousin, Ann. She loved ranch dressing with garlic, loved caramel. They all liked sweet popcorn rather than salty. I like it as salty as possible. Ramona had already experienced ulcers at her young age.

I found out that on Sunday it was forbidden to mow the lawn between one and three in the afternoon. Mark, my dad in Wisconsin, never mowed the lawn on a Sunday—ever. It was *verboten*. Dieter said that one to three was considered siesta time and people were to use quiet voices. Also, Dieter had to keep telling me to watch out for bicycles. The bicyclists had their very own lane (on the sidewalk) and their very own miniature traffic lights. I kept stepping into that lane and forgetting to look both ways. In Germany, bikes have first priority; then cars, then people. Berlin has superior mass transit for its people. The double-decker buses and the UBahn were great for getting around when Ramona and I went sightseeing.

Dieter told me that Klaus was a hypochondriac. He was always complaining about this ailment or that. He would say he was not hungry or thirsty and then have three helpings. *Yikes. I saw a lot of me in Klaus and Erika, and I didn't want to end up as fat as either of them. I promised myself I'd go on a diet when I got home.* Klaus and I, besides having the same color eyes, had so many mannerisms that were strikingly similar. Things I can't put into words. Klaus always talked with his hands, as I do. Even the way he told a story was the same. He loved the actual telling of it, as I do. *I only wish I knew what he was saying.*

Helga studied my face when she thought I was not looking. *Certainly I am not like her. I hoped.* Her cool demeanor was countered by Klaus' overfriendliness. Each day she would wear the heart pin I had given her when I first came to her apartment, and that was a nice gesture. One day she wore a very low-cut top and it made her look like a 66-year-old hooker. Her hair was dyed bright magenta, a color I saw many German women sporting. I wore the pearl stick pin she gave me and the black and white scarf.

Poor Eszter, it seemed all she did was work. I felt guilty not helping her with meals, but the kitchen was very small and there was no room. She knew just what she wanted to do and how she wanted to do it. If she was home she made a big breakfast, then tea later in the afternoon and then a huge supper. Of course, we had some leftovers and that was always fine with me. She cooked for four people for two weeks and worked part-time on top of that. Ramona was a big help to her if she wasn't at the university or working part-time at the bank. They were definitely a very close-knit family. One thing we discovered—we all loved sweets.

There were so many things that made them laugh at me—in a good-natured way. For instance, I could not figure out how to lock (and then unlock) the bathroom door at the weekend house. I would try and try and then Dieter would come and show me again. I finally got it after many, many tries. Meantime they noticed that I went to the bathroom a lot, and apparently so did Erika and Ramona, and Helga. We guessed it was genetic. *Why didn't I inherit a gene that made me learn languages with ease?*

At the weekend house we sang. Dieter played the guitar and Klaus played the keyboard. Dieter played the keyboard too, without knowing how to read music. And, of course, he played the accordion. I tried to show off my skill at "playing the spoons," but Klaus laughed at my poor attempt and took them away. He called it *loffel polka*—spoon polka. It was so much fun. Klaus would try to tell a joke, half in English and half in German. At the end of the joke, he would wait for me to laugh and couldn't understand why I didn't. One time he told me a whole joke in broken English and I told him, "Sorry, Klaus, but I didn't understand it." So, he started to tell me again, this time in German.

"Klaus," I said. "If I didn't understand it in English I won't understand it in German." And then we all laughed again—and again—throughout the evening. *I could hear myself laughing with my brothers and my sister, my niece and my lovely sister-in-law. It was too wonderful to comprehend at the time. By the end of that day at the weekend house I had learned a huge amount about my family, but I knew that the main reason I would return to Germany was because of Dieter.*

My brother, Dieter, always hugging me,
so thrilled we found each other.

Soup's on! At Dieter's garden house.

Chapter Twenty-Eight

A Visit of Wonder

I loved Eszter's infectious laugh. She was so genuine and friendly and made me feel so welcome. If I had stayed with Helga in her apartment I know I would have been miserable.

I learned from Helga that apparently Gerhard had another child—a girl—from when he went to live in the Black Forest after the war. This was after divorcing my mother, although none of them knew about their divorce back then. Dieter confirmed that he, too, knew about the other daughter, but he didn't know how he knew. Helga said she overheard Gerhard and Erika arguing and Erika yelled, "If you don't like it here, go to your daughter in the Black Forest." Helga laughed, *"Die ganze familie ist fezerruck."* Translation: The whole family is crazy.

We talked about the fact that Gerhard always looked younger than his actual age. Dieter did too until he lost most of his hair. *Many times, over the years, people told me that I looked younger than whatever age I currently was.* None of us, my siblings nor I, had wrinkles early. *More and more while I was in Germany I thought, "I am Gerhard's child."* Helga did not want me to do DNA testing. She thought that Dieter should just tell me that Gerhard was my father and that should end it.

Dieter told me that he didn't love Gerhard, but that he didn't want to regret anything after Gerhard was gone, so he made peace with him. He said that as children they were afraid of him and that my mother was a little bit, too. Erika was under his thumb and Gerhard always told her what to do and when to do it. Sometimes she would rebel. Dieter said Erika enjoyed her life after Gerhard was gone. She traveled and had many friends.

Often Dieter and Eszter would call me Erika because I was always writing notes about things, which apparently my mama did, too. She was writing all the time about anything and everything. *Was my desire and love of writing something I inherited from my birth mother? In retrospect, the fact that I did take notes through my whole visit is why I'm able to write this memoir. That very full notebook and my emails to Jim were what put the whole picture together for me now, 18 years later.*

Dieter and I got up very early one morning and had yet another big breakfast. Then we were off to the government offices for my birth certificate. Once again, something was still not right. The paper she had in front of her said Gerda Erika *Elliot*. I never had any paperwork that put those three names together. She told Dieter that she believed that I was this person, but I did not have a paper to prove it. Finally, Dieter told her the whole story. She said if there was not a question of *proving for inheritance*, then she would give him a copy.

"What inheritance?" Dieter asked. "My mama and papa are dead and the adoption papers say she has no legal right to anything with the Paul name." Thirty minutes later we had the copy. We hurried out of there as quickly as we could. Mission accomplished. Now I had all the pieces of paper that identified me all through the years of my life. And now, officially, I had seven different names.

After many days in Germany, I'd been trying so hard to speak German that I started to have trouble remembering the English words for things. It affected my writing to Jim in English. On the 12th of September I wrote to him, "Ramona turns off the computer *for so not electricity*."

Ramona laughed at me because everywhere she took me—Checkpoint Charlie, the Brandenburg Gate, The Wall, Under den Linden (the most famous street in East Berlin)—I wanted to buy souvenirs. She said Dieter was just like that.

I wrote to Jim, *"Dieter told me this morning that although we have only known each other for six days, he feels we have known each other all our lives. I feel that way, too. He is the older brother I always wanted."*

He had curly hair (when he had hair) and he loved to stay up late. Ramona told me he always waits till the last minute and then rushes to get somewhere on time, but is never a minute late. I wished he would quit smoking. Now that I had found him, I didn't want to lose him. A few years later he did quit, and so did Ramona. I had quit 12 years earlier.

Dieter loved *The X-Files* and *Star Trek*, mysteries with *Colombo* and *Murder She Wrote*, and he did *not* like scary shows. We were truly *like two peas in a pod—like two left slippers.* Dieter and I approach people in the same way—warmly. We're both upfront people, usually asking rather than telling people. *Well, unless you ask my husband, then you might get a different version of my claim.*

Each night we would all take our places on the chairs and couches in Dieter's living room. We would talk, eat, and laugh. And talk, eat, and tell stories which again poor Ramona had to work hard to interpret. I was getting better about communicating in German, but not for long stories. Those I needed to tell in English. I would speak for about five minutes, then Ramona would interpret. Then I would speak for another five minutes. They were still struggling with the reality of Erika and Gerhard being divorced in 1946 and then remarrying right before I was born in 1948. We decided that Erika must have had an affair and gotten pregnant and Dieter said he could see Gerhard saying, *"I will come home and marry you and take care of the other children—my children—but not this one that is not mine."* Dieter said he could imagine Erika agreeing to do that. She was not a terribly strong person and would have taken the easy way out.

A day later was the anniversary of Mama's death. We went to the cemetery again and put flowers on her grave. I had trouble looking at her grave and feeling much of anything. I loved hearing the stories and finding out that I had a family that was so much like me, but she knew she was dying and she never told the family about me. Eszter thinks

Erika didn't tell anyone because Eszter, whose sister had adopted a child, would often say, *"How could anyone give up their child?"*

Also, Eszter said that Erika never visited her in the hospital when she had Ramona. Eszter thinks, in hindsight, that it might have been because it reminded her of giving me up at birth. That was touching, but not too relevant to me at age 52. Years later, when my daughter got married, she asked me if I wanted my birth parents' names on the wedding program. Without one second of thought I burst out, "No, absolutely not. They gave me away, they don't deserve to be mentioned." *Wow, even now I'm kind of surprised at my outburst.*

Dieter took me to Buddestrasse, which was where Anna Müller (my maternal grandmother) had an apartment in "former times." (often Dieter or Ramona would refer to the past as "former times"). We walked the streets and I drank in the culture and scenery. He told me about how frugal Mama had to be. She made cake from coffee grounds and used potato skins and burned flour to make soup. Rabbit, pork, and beef were available, but not to everyone all the time. Mustard was unheard of. They never saw white bread. She also spoke a little English. *(I wonder if it could have been from meeting Dorothy, my first adoptive mother.)* Hearing that soldiers went through every house in the Russian sector sent chills through me.

People would leave blankets on the front steps in hopes they would take them and not come in. What a different life they had growing up in East Berlin. This could have been my hometown; my neighborhood. The kids and Mama lived there during the war. He showed me the building where my maternal grandmother's apartment was. It was a beautiful old, ornate apartment building on a corner. There were balconies full of flowers. I pictured Dieter and the others skipping along the cobblestones, playing hide-and-seek, getting into trouble.

That night I took everyone to dinner at the restaurant called Split Grill. The food was wonderful and we all toasted with *Psertizg Schnaps*. I didn't normally drink, but the occasion was pretty special. Helga warmed up a little after several drinks and suddenly, without warning, she grabbed my hand and put a pretty gold ring with a pink stone on my finger. Years before, Gerhard had given both her and my mother a ring from Russia. The stone was alexandrite—a pinkish stone in a filigreed gold setting. Helga had given one of the two rings to a friend but got it back when she learned about me. She had been waiting for an appropriate time to present it to me.

I started to cry, and she started to cry, and then Klaus started to cry, and then Dieter and Eszter and Ramona cried. The waiter must have thought we were all nuts. I paid the bill with Visa, but it didn't have a line on it for a tip, and I totally forgot to tip. When I remembered later, I found out Helga had done it for me. I was so embarrassed and, of course, I reimbursed her. The saddest part of that evening was that Detti was not able to come and I didn't know why. I was very worried that I might not see him again and never get photos of all of us together.

I had sent packages to everyone before I left for Germany, but some were late in showing up. Jim was tracking them from home, but they were just not arriving. Dieter said he was born on a Sunday, and anyone born on a Sunday is lucky. It was true because we were leaving the next day to go somewhere and the mail lady was in the vestibule by the mailboxes. Dieter asked her if there was anything for him. "No," she said.

"What is that package in your arms?" Dieter replied.

"Oh, it's a mistake. It has your address on it, but the person's name is Bonnie Willemssen." He told her, "This is my sister Bonnie Willemssen, and she sent it to herself at this address." Apparently you never do that in Germany because they only deliver to the person whose name is on the *mailbox*. I told him in America you can have any name on the package as long as the address is correct. The reason I had put my name on it was so they wouldn't open it before I got there. We warned Helga that the packages I sent to her had *my* name on them. It all got straightened out and all packages came. In the end, everyone got their gifts and souvenirs.

I asked Helga that night when she might like to come visit me in Wisconsin. She said, "*Morgen*."

Tomorrow? Yikes! I had hoped to learn a lot more German before she came to visit so we could communicate better. I had so many questions to ask her about Mama. Turned out Helga was the first one to come visit me the following spring. Ramona suspected Helga wanted to make sure she was the first so she could tell all the others what our house and lives were like.

Dieter loved his Mercedes. If a German citizen waited for a new car to be a year old they could get it for half price. He took me to the Mercedes show room. Wow, what a beautiful structure—several floors of glass showcasing shiny new cars. I knew that Jim would love to explore there, but all I bought him was a Mercedes keychain. When I emailed about that excursion, Jim got all excited. He wanted me to buy a Mercedes and bring it home. Ha! He even went to the dealership in Wisconsin to find out about that possibility.

The cars they make for Germany do not have the emission standards required in the U.S., so by the time you add those on to be acceptable to be transferred to the States, you might as well buy the car in the States. What I personally fell in love with were the Smart Cars. They were adorable little things that were as wide as they were long. You could park the front wheels against the curb and not take up any more room than if you parallel parked. I would have loved to pack one of those in my suitcase and bring it home. A few years later Smart Cars made their way to the USA.

Breakfast with Dieter. We are eating "Klaus heads"
– our little joke about Klaus' big bald head.

I took everyone out to the Split Grill
– Detti was not feeling well enough to join us.

Me at dinner.

Helga at dinner.

Klaus, enjoying his drink.

Chapter Twenty–Nine

Time is Passing

I continued to learn about my family as the days passed. Klaus seemed to be a "mooch." He took off his watch after one meal and said he liked my watch. The rest of them scolded him.

"Gerda knows I only make a little joke."

How would I know that? When I took them all out to dinner, I asked Klaus if he would like another drink and his answer was, "If you are buying, I am drinking." He never had much as far as money or material things, so I guess I understood. He thought I was a rich relative who was going to change his life.

Dieter talked about the air raids and the bombing and how lucky I was to have lived in America. He was right. From his point of view, I'd been very lucky. *But, while he was with his blood relatives, I was not. I was in America wondering who my family might be. Who just gives away a child? Somehow, in my heart, I knew I had a brother. I believe that at the times I felt the loneliest, that is when Dieter thought of America.*

Dieter remembered Mama sending him to the corner tavern for a carton of watery soup with one carrot in it for supper. My life in Wisconsin was going out to eat with my older, established parents. It was piano, guitar, voice, and art lessons, Brownies and Girl Scouting, and owning two horses. It was tennis and golf at the country club and long trips each year. It was new Easter bonnets and Christmas outfits and proper clothes for each event in my life. But it was also learning to be a "good girl" and not make Mother angry. It was always walking on eggshells and never expressing my real opinion for fear of offending her. It was never being allowed to show any emotion—sadness, anger, or even joy.

Mother believed it was never a good idea to get too excited about things like trips, holidays, or a birthday. It might not happen and then you will be disappointed. I think that disappointment may have been a large part of her youth. There were times I had to tune out my brain so that it didn't melt when my frustration was so great I thought I would explode. I spent many hours of my younger life wishing I had not been separated from my birth family and wondering if I had any siblings and if they knew about me.

Dieter and I went to the *Tegalersee* (Tegal Sea) and took a two-hour boat ride on a boat that was painted to look like a whale. It held 400 people, so it was huge. It was a beautiful sunny, warm day and Dieter continued telling me more about his childhood. I could have listened forever. He said it was possible to go any place in Berlin from the water, and even to the Danube and the Baltic Sea, Sweden, and Poland. I learned that when The Wall was up people were sometimes allowed to go across the border to see family if someone was sick or if it was a special occasion, but they were never allowed to cross as a whole family at the same time.

Ramona and Eszter had Hungarian passports, so Dieter would go through the line about ten people ahead of his wife and child. The guards were never the wiser, and then the three of them could visit Helga and enjoy "the other side." When he was young, Dieter ice skated on the Tegal Sea and sailed on it when he was older. He spent three years in the navy—a good match for his love of water.

Until The Wall went up in 1961, Dieter sailed many times on the Wanasee to West Berlin. He said he would have loved a sailboat after he was married, and always had a sailing license, but Eszter said no because she did not know how to swim. After he was finished with his time in the navy he was offered a chance to be on a 4,000-passenger vessel as a musician and mechanic, but he said no because he was homesick for Berlin. He always kept his sailing license current, however.

We ate lunch on the boat. Dieter showed me how to cross my knife and fork when I was finished eating. Sure enough, the waiter took my plate but left Dieter's because he was still eating. *Think that would happen at Olive Garden?*

After the boat ride we walked the streets of the Tegal district. Dieter had many good memories of visiting his/our *Oma* Anna there. I was happy to know he had some good memories. *I was feeling very sorry for my family and the lives they had been forced to live because of the war, the Russians, and the poverty.*

It was interesting that my German family had special shoes for wearing inside the house. The second they crossed the threshold, they exchanged outdoor shoes for indoor shoes, even in their garden house. I had not brought "indoor shoes," so I went barefoot or left on my socks. Dieter was aghast. *"No one should go barefoot because they will get a cold in their kidneys."* I'm not sure how the two were related, but he was adamant. I just laughed and assured him I would not get a cold in my kidneys.

I think we both knew we needed to get to know each other well and only had a short amount of time. More ways we were alike: We both got migraines. Dieter loved Doris Day, loved to dance, and always wanted other people to feel comfortable (definitely a trait I possess). He speaks before he thinks, and I've been accused of that, too.

Whenever he would come back to the apartment it would take my breath away. My heart would do a little flip. I loved this positive guy who always saw the glass half full instead of half empty, again something I always did. We both seem to possess an ESP ability which was kind of eerie to hear someone else say they possessed too.

Chapter Thirty

Sunshine in the Morning

Dieter was always so happy and cheerful. Even when he didn't get much sleep he was in a good mood. I always thought that perhaps I was born with a "happy" spoon in my mouth, instead of a "silver" one. I'm able to see the positive side of things no matter how life turns. Dieter said to me that I was like "sunshine in the morning," and it made me very proud that he approved of me, of my personality, and that he liked me. He really did have the cutest way of saying things. Ramona, on the other hand, was not a morning person. She reminded me so much of Ann it was unbelievable. Ramona definitely didn't want to cheerily chat in the morning like Dieter and I did.

I asked Ramona if she would like to come visit us in La Crosse the following summer. She was thrilled and said she would do all she could to make it happen. I knew she would be a very good house guest. In order for her to come visit us for six weeks, she needed to secure an application and prove to the German government that she had a job in America. Jim, who owned a business at the time, created a job for her and then wrote letters asking for her to come to do an internship. She did not actually work for him because she and I had *much more important things to do*. At the end of her visit Jim wrote a letter of recommendation on his letter-head stationary that she could take back to her government.

One of the days I was in Berlin Ramona took me to the *Kudam*, short for *Kurfurstadam Strasse*. We walked along that large, wonderful street with all its expensive shops. In 1962, with Mary and Mark, we stayed on the *Kurfurstadam Strasse*—at the Berlin Hilton. Jimmy Stewart and his family were there. The desk clerk told us what floor Mr. Stewart was on and my mother insisted that she and I stake out his floor till he came to the elevator. When we got on the elevator with him, Mother made me pretend that I was the one that wanted his autograph.

On that trip, we were only able to go into East Berlin on a day tour bus. In those days a minor child in the United States (I was 12) could be on the same passport photo as the parent. My picture and name were on my mother's passport, but it did not list my birthplace, if it had, I would not have been allowed into the Eastern Sector of the city. What my adoptive father worried about the most was that they might not let me *out* again after the tour. He commanded me not to say *a single word* as the East German guards came through the bus when we passed through Checkpoint Charlie. If asked where I was born, I was to lie and say La Crosse, Wisconsin. He was so nervous that whole day, and only breathed a sigh of relief when we were safely back in West Berlin. Not until years later, when I had a child of my own, did I fully understand his fear.

On that bus, however, I was busy studying the faces of the few women we saw scurrying on the quiet streets. I was looking for anyone who could be my mother—someone who looked just like me. The tour guide escorted us to many memorials that day, often telling us of how wonderfully the Russians were taking care of the area, and to notice how much reconstruction was going on. Later we heard that the guides on the bus told each tour group that it was a holiday that day, and that was why we didn't see any people working.

That flight in 1962 took us to Tempelhof Airport. When Dieter drove me to their apartment on my first morning, we drove past Tempelhof. I recognized the famous sculpture outside. Dieter said Tempelhof was now a local airport. Each day, as we drove through the streets of Berlin I thought of what could have been.

I could have lived in this city, been brought up here, and been imprisoned here for nearly thirty years like my brothers and my sister and my parents. My birth family had been walled up here. They had endured their loss of freedom at the whim of an egotistical country. Was I lucky to have been adopted and not have had to grow up here? Was I sad about being adopted and not growing up with my natural family? I had my answer by the time I returned to America.

One night we went to Helga's for dinner. I was relieved to learn that all five of us would be there. Dieter and I picked up Detti at his apartment. On the way to Helga's, we sang songs from a mixed tape Dieter had made. Detti had a beautiful voice. Sitting in the front seat, listening to him, he sounded just like Elvis. *It gave me chills. Plus, I was singing in the car with my brothers. It was surreal.* Dieter was always telling me little tidbits of information about his life and their lives. During the drive, he told me that Gerhard gave Mama ten marks every day. It was for household expenses.

I can describe Detti as barely pulling himself together. He wore his weird hat plunked on long, greasy hair—the same hat that was present when I met him at the airport. I think the rest of the family was embarrassed by his appearance and wished he would have cleaned up a little bit more. He apparently told Dieter that he didn't want to pretend to be someone he wasn't with me. *Have to respect that.*

That night I was with all four of my siblings in the same room. My mind was starting to break apart again. I seemed unable to just be in the moment—it was too much to take in. After dinner, Helga had a neighbor come over and take a few—too few—photos of the five of us, and they were the only photos I will ever have of my siblings and I in the same room. My next trip, three years later, I saw all of them, but not all in the same place for a group photo. I will always regret that I didn't insist on more photos.

Before dinner, Detti asked the others to leave the room so he could speak to me privately, completely in German, for twenty minutes. I had no idea what he said, but there were tears in his eyes. He seemed very heartfelt, as if he was pouring his heart out to me. He gave me some gifts;

nothing momentous but they were from my brother and that made them meaningful. I wish I knew what he said to me. I never will.

When we got back to the Paul apartment, Dieter gave me a small brass perpetual calendar that Gerhard and Erika had owned. He said it was always on their mantle. He had kept it as a memento and now wanted me to have it. It was set to July 30, 1948—my birthday. *I didn't have the nerve to ask who had set that date on it. I wanted to pretend Erika had done it.*

Jim wrote to tell me of his adventures back home. Ramona sent him a German sentence to translate, and he tried. He told me to tell her that if it's not right, he will have to come over to Germany and help her with her German.

He kept the house going during my absence. He was missing me. I was missing him. As much as I loved my trip, it was getting hard not to hear English spoken around me. I was starting to feel isolated, especially around Helga. Sometimes I just drifted off in my own thoughts, usually thinking of home and what was happening in my classes at the university while I was gone.

One of my last nights in Berlin we ate dinner at the apartment. Eszter's cooking was wonderful as always. We watched home movies of some of the Paul trips. So often they'd tell me I reminded them of Erika. I wasn't sure if I felt complimented or not, although I know they thought it was special. We went through some old family papers that Dieter had found packed away. While we were sitting there, Dieter discovered, by reading Helga's birth certificate, that Mama was six months pregnant when she got married the first time. Another new discovery. It seemed like a daily event while I was there. The final night, the four of us went to a Chinese restaurant. I know it's silly to say, but it was so odd to hear Chinese people speaking German.

Our last night – Chinese restaurant.

Chapter Thirty-One

The First Goodbye

It was the day before I was to fly back to Wisconsin. There were last-minute things to do: packing, showering, and saying goodbye to everyone except Detti (who I only saw two times). As I look back on the trip, I wish I would have insisted that I see Detti one more time, and that we try one more time for pictures of all of us. Three years later on my next trip (with Jim, this time) we were not able to all be together because Klaus was in Frankfurt and no one wanted to host him in their apartment. I thought of paying for a hotel room for Klaus but decided against it—a decision I regret now because Detti died shortly after our visit in 2003. The photo opportunity for a decent picture of the five of us died with him.

I had Dieter take me to a store where I could buy a German hair dryer and German curling iron for my next trip. Then I wouldn't have to bring a converter. We made more copies of pictures, and of his accordion music. I always liked accordion players at Oktoberfest both in La Crosse and in Munich. It must have been my German ancestors' musical blood in my veins.

I wrote and told Jim that if the plane crashed, I wanted him to buy Dieter a silver ID bracelet and have it inscribed with *Dieter and Bonnie—two left slippers.* I said that I felt that a piece of my heart would stay with

Dieter. I cared for the others, but most especially Dieter. Over the next few years, I would grow to love sweet, sensitive Detti who died much too early, and silly, crazy Klaus who died in 2016.

Helga and I never warmed up to each other, although I know she was thrilled by my existence and happy to have a sister. Perhaps as the oldest and the one who had the most responsibility, she envied me more than loved me. It's okay. We found each other before she passed away in 2007.

We all stayed up until 3 a.m. talking that night. It was going to be hard to go back to my "real" world. I realized I was a wife, a mother, a teacher, and now a sister.

Dieter called *Tante* Sophie. She was my mama's first cousin and best friend. Dieter asked her —again—if she would tell him what happened in regard to my birth. He had called her earlier and told her about me, but she refused to meet me. This time she told him that she would not speak ill of the dead, but that Erika and Gerhard did not want to have another child. *Was it as simple as that? Did they know I was their child, but they just didn't want to raise another child in a one-bedroom apartment with so little food and money?*

Ramona's email to Jim:

"Dear Jim! Unfortunately Bonnie left us now. We are a bit sad about that, but we hope we will meet you all soon. We brought her to the airport; don't forget to pick her up. Try again writing German sentences. It was always good what you write and we had a lot to laugh about. Please tell Bonnie that the visitor's platform at the airport was closed so we couldn't wave our hands to her so we watched her start from another glass tower, but I am sure she couldn't see us. All the best. Bonnie we miss you!!! Lovingly, the 3 Pauls."

My email to my family in Germany:

"Hi – I cannot begin to tell you how wonderful my time was with all of you. You have become so very important to me. Never will we be far apart in heart and soul – although by necessity sometimes in body. I will write more when I can think straight. The fights were all fine. I think I did quite well holding back my tears – I love you all – Eszter, how can I exist without you and Ramona sitting every night with me and quawtching *(chatting)? Love, Bonnie"*

Ramona playing the accordion.

Dieter playing the accordion.

Mama playing the accordion.

One last goodbye at the airport.

Chapter Thirty–Two

Reality Steps In

It was good to be back home but hard to get into my old, regular routine. My days had been spent learning about my birth family and my homeland. My nights were filled with love and laughter. Now life was back to normal. I had to start teaching two days after getting home. I didn't feel prepared, but my boss, who had substituted in my classes for me, came up with a clever way to teach a Language Arts concept and have me educate the students about where I had been and why I missed the first two weeks of the semester. For this lesson, she asked me to write a one-page summary of my experiences. I titled it "Like Two Left Slippers." I think the students were both fascinated by my story and forgave my absence.

Ramona and I continued to write to each other by email. She and her parents were flying to Florida in a few weeks. I wished I had some time off for Jim and me to go there to see them, but there was no way. They were obsessed with hot weather. It was never warm enough in Berlin for them, even in the summer. All they wanted to do was sit in a swimming pool and bake in the sun.

I had left some little gifts for Dieter and Ramona when I left. I gave Dieter my electronic translator. I also left the Euros I had left and more jewelry for Ramona. She worried at first that I had forgotten it, but I assured her that I had left it for her. My brother had made a copy of many of his videos from family trips. He sent it back with me, but unfortunately it did not work in our VCR. I spent a small fortune having someone convert it for me.

Over the next few months we planned for them to visit Wisconsin. I wanted to show my hometown to them and have them meet my friends and family.

Ramona wrote that they were all so glad that I had stayed with them and not in a hotel. *"When you stay in a hotel you possibly had more comfort, but we wouldn't know each other as much as now and we couldn't spend such a lovely time together."*

I answered her the next day. *"You are so very right about not getting to know each other as well if I had stayed at a hotel. I would have loved for Jim to see and hear and be part of all that I experienced but this was a journey that I had to make alone and he knew that and so did I. Staying with you was the best way to get to know each other and oh boy, did we have a great time. And so many, many laughs! I miss our late night 'gab' sessions till 1:00 in the morning, and "chocolate eating binges."'*

Ramona laughed when she said that Dieter had forgotten his Hungarian when he was chatting with Eszter's relatives on the phone and was using his English instead. I told her to tell Eszter that I actually lost a few pounds on the trip, so chocolate, crème, cake, and desserts must be good for me.

On September 22, 2000, I wrote to Ramona.

"My life is forever changed by finding my family. Words are hard to find to express how wonderful I feel now that I have all of you in my life. Knowing my roots has been such an uplifting experience. I must have repressed my desire for birth family for a long time, not feeling or acknowledging that I needed to find you, and when I did find you it was like a dam burst. Remember that we all have Ann to thank for finally getting me to start my search and basically I did it for her – so that she could have medical knowledge. Never in my wildest dreams did I expect you all to want to know me and to actually love me. I

thought that if I found any sisters and brothers they would simply say, "Well, you are the half-sister and we are interested in you but that is all." This has been so much better than my expectations – I had a wonderful dream and it came true."

Later in the same email:

"How can I ever thank you for your hospitality? Eszter opened her home for two weeks to a stranger and she cooked and cleaned and served and washed dishes and always with a smile. She stayed up late at night to talk when she had to get up early and work and she came home from work and started working again when she would have liked to rest. And you, Ramona, had to give up your room for two weeks, live with things scattered everywhere and you had no place to get away from everyone for a little while. You did endless interpreting and made conversation between Eszter and you and me joyful and you gave up your time to take me places (and got sore feet in the bargain). You made me feel welcome and warm, you made me feel loved, you made me feel that you were happy I found you, and for that I will be forever grateful. I will remember those two weeks as the best two weeks ever.

Dieter, for you I have only a loving heart. I cannot believe how much alike you and I are. I cry for the life you lived—difficult, frightening, and dangerous. And I applaud how wonderfully you turned out despite an abusive father and meager circumstances in your childhood. You have been the HEAD of the family—the one that everyone else turned to for support both emotionally and physically. You are strong and you have a quiet presence that instills confidence. From the moment I met you I knew that I trusted you. I knew you were a good man and I knew that you were the big brother I always wanted and needed. And, as we say in America "better late than never."

You have filled a hole in my heart that was always there and I think already I am better for having found you. There is so much I do not know about you and yet I feel that I have known you forever – that somehow the 'imprint' of you was always with me, somewhere in my being. I know this is getting beyond your English skills but I feel that I need to express myself in English. I will try German later. You are very sweet. I loved it when you hugged me and called me 'Sunshine." The smile on your face and the love in your eyes will stay in my memory forever. You are my brother—half or whole makes no difference to me – you are my BIG brother, my BEST BIG BROTHER. I wish for us many, many, many years together so that we can make up for all the years we were apart.

Love to all of you, and especially to my "Other Left Slipper." Bonnie"

Chapter Thirty-Three

Dorothy

It was late September of 2000. I was home from my momentous trip to meet my birth family, but there were still many questions that needed an answer. Why did Erika and Gerhard give me up? How did they know Dorothy? Where did Dorothy go after she gave me up?

I had one clue. In 1977, after our baby died, my adoptive parents tried to find Dorothy. They called the phone number they still had for her from all the years before when they adopted me. They called that number and got through to Dorothy's son, who told them Dorothy had passed away. Walter's strong German accent was difficult for Mary to understand on the phone so he told Mary to call Clara, his wife.

Mary saw no point in doing that because if Dorothy was dead, any chance of knowing about birth family medical history was probably long gone. Mary did not realize that Clara was my former nurse/nanny, the quiet woman who had been my nanny for four years and had sat with them on the *SS United States* all those years ago. Clara had ended up marrying Dorothy's son who was my Godfather according to my baptismal certificate.

I had only been home a few weeks from Berlin. DNA testing was still in the waiting stage, but I was curious to know more about Dorothy.

Mostly I wanted to know if her family might know anything about my birth mother and whether we might of all lived in the same apartment building in Berlin.

I called the number still in Mary's records. A man with an accent answered. It was Dorothy's son Walter, and he was very pleased to hear from me when I identified myself. He told me to call Clara and gave me her phone number. Thinking that she might speak better English, I was happy to be passed off to her. I called her and told her who I was. She was incredulous. She could not believe it was me and that I was calling her.

I didn't realize, at this time, that she was my nanny from my early years. She cried and so I cried, too. It seemed to be the thing to do throughout the past year. Her accent was thick, also. I clutched the phone so hard and tried to hear and write down everything she was telling me. She was so excited and therefore was speaking way too fast for me to catch it all. She told me she had been my nanny. It was my turn to be surprised. *Here was the connection to my health history that could have helped me, and we never knew it.*

If only Mary had made that extra phone call in 1977 some of this might have been explained. Clara told me that we (Dorothy, me, and Clara) traveled a lot to accommodate Dorothy's job. Clara spoke of Dorothy having had another daughter who died of TB or diphtheria but I'm not sure I got the whole picture although, I thought I remembered something like that from the letter Dorothy had written to me when I was in high school. Clara didn't know anything about my birth family, but, of course, having just traveled back from meeting them, that was not as important to me at the moment.

My goal now was to connect the dots from my birth through four years and to my voyage to the USA. Clara told me she had pictures. *Pictures? Oh my God!* Was it possible that I might get to see myself at the age of one or two? Luckily I did have four pictures that Dorothy gave to Mary, but that was all. Mary filled bucketfuls of albums after I came to live with them. I asked Clara if she would make copies of her photos and send them to me. She said, "Yes, of course, they are of you." I was in 7th Heaven. We chatted a bit more. I told her about being in Germany to meet my brothers and my sister, and she was happy for me. Some of the information she revealed to me was that we all lived in Frankfurt-am-Main, at least in 1951. My *Reisepass* (passport) had my name and a photo. It said my eyes were *braun*. There is a stamp that says I was admitted to the United States on June 15, 1952.

At one point there was a girl named Monica, perhaps another child that Dorothy adopted. Clara talked about both of us having arms in a cast at the same time, and that we all flew from Berlin to Nuremberg on a plane from England because Clara was not allowed to fly on an American plane. I'm not sure why. Perhaps because she was not an American citizen and it was just after the war. She says we lived in an apartment house in Berlin. *Could it have been the same one that Mama and my siblings lived in?* I gave her the address of the one Dieter thought we all lived in but it did not seem familiar to her.

She said that her husband had a sister and a brother. She talked about her two children. She said they (she and Dorothy) always thought I had an American father—probably a soldier. I told her that yes, Dorothy had indicated that in the letter she sent to me back when I was in high school. She said, in Germany at that time, having an American father was a terrible thing.

Clara told me that Dorothy remarried her husband (the one she had divorced in the 40s.) after she returned to the U.S. She claimed that Dorothy's "mind was good" but that she was "a little bit flighty and impulsive." There was no love from Dorothy's wealthy family. Clara said that Dorothy wanted to be an actress, but her mother sent her to boarding school in Switzerland for art school instead.

Dorothy was a great skier and had many ski jumping trophies. She traveled to Switzerland when she was about 70 and had a stroke there but lived until she was 78. When I asked Clara where she thought Dorothy and Erika might have met, she said she thought in an office—*Ig Farben*. Clara thought that they might have worked together, but she was not sure how that could have been with Dorothy being a nurse. Clara said Dorothy mentioned that one of the secretaries in the office had a baby, but none of my siblings ever remember Mama working in an office.

We said we'd talk again. I called Clara about a week later. Her attitude had changed. I couldn't quite figure out what was different. She seemed cautious—less enthusiastic to talk with me. I asked more questions and she almost whispered the answers. I asked her if there was a problem and she said that "he" didn't want her to talk to me. *He? Walter? husband* I tried to ask her who and why and what was the problem, but I could tell she wanted to get off the phone.

I called her again in a week and didn't get an answer. I called the other phone number—her husband Walter's number. A man answered, and I asked for Walter. He asked me who was calling and I told him my name. His reply was, "I'm his son and I don't want you talking to my parents anymore." *What? What did I do? What was wrong?* Walter and Clara both sounded so happy to hear from me in the beginning. *What was it?* I wondered briefly if the grandchildren were worried I wanted to try to collect an inheritance. I wanted to call the son back and reassure him that I was not interested in their business assets—a deli and catering business—but his voice was very forbidding.

I waited months to call again. Clara answered. I asked her yet again for the photos of me. She agreed but seemed frail. I said I'd send a SASE so all she had to do was put them in the envelope and put them in the mailbox. She sounded unsure and timid and old. *Was there something wrong with her?* I sent the envelope, but no photos were sent to my house. I waited months to call again. This time a woman answered. I asked to speak to Clara and she said Clara was very sick and could not answer the phone. I asked her if she was the caregiver. She said, "No, I'm her daughter."

I explained who I was and told her about my conversation with her brother and asked if she felt the same way. The daughter said she did not know about the earlier call but did not feel that way. However, Clara was dying and she would not be able to talk to me again. We continued chatting briefly. She thought that perhaps her brother was projecting the feeling that had been prevalent around their family dinner table—that I had been "stolen" from Dorothy. Dorothy had led her family to believe that Mary and Mark had taken advantage of her lack of husband, family, and roots and had "stolen" me away from her. I was shocked to hear that. One thing I knew for sure was that Mary and Mark were always aboveboard about everything in their lives.

They believed they would never get into Heaven unless they lived a good life. I can assure you that if any two people would be zooming right through the Pearly Gates after death, it would be both of them. I didn't know what to say. Should I tell Clara's daughter the truth? I had lots of letters to back it up. Instead, I asked if I could call and check on Clara's condition in a few weeks. She agreed.

The next time I called, the daughter answered. Clara's condition had deteriorated even more. I asked her if she knew if there were any pictures of me. "Oh, yes," she said, "I've seen those pictures. I'm not sure where they are right now, but they should be yours." *Yes.* I breathed a sigh of relief. She was willing to get me the photos. "Would you send them to me?" I asked

"Yes, but not until Mother is gone and I have time to go through everything." *Well, I'd waited half a century for them. I could wait a little longer.*

Clara died. I spoke again with the daughter. No, she had not looked for the pictures, but she would.

"How about this?" I said. "After you send me the pictures I'll send you the original letters written by your grandmother to my mother. There are about ten or fifteen of them."

I realized that although I'd hung on to them through the years, they didn't mean anything to me except for their content. I had copies. She could have the originals. I waited and waited for the daughter to mail me some photos. Months passed. I would forget about them and then something would remind me. I hoped that she would send them, but she didn't.

After a year, I decided I'd make a bolder move. I gathered all the original letters from Dorothy, Mary's responses to her, and also copies of Mary and Mark's separate letters written on the night they returned from Delaware with me so many years before. I sent the original photos my mother had of Dorothy, including the one of her with me and the doctor she was traveling with on the ship. I sent it Fed Ex. I told Fed Ex that I wanted someone to sign for them. I waited and I kept checking for some indication that the papers had been received. In tracking them through Fed Ex I discovered that they had not gotten a signature for the package, but had instead left it at a different address than what was on the envelope.

The man at the counter in La Crosse could not explain to me why that happened. I was so distraught that I nearly had a meltdown in the store. I could not contemplate that papers that I had had in my possession for over 50 years could disappear. Of course I had copies, but this was my bargaining chip with Dorothy's granddaughter and now it was gone. I decided I had to call the granddaughter to see if she might have gotten the package. Thank Heaven, she *did* receive it. I was so relieved. I asked her what she thought of the letters.

"I'm in shock. I am still processing it."

"Well," I said, "I would sure appreciate those photos after you have processed this." We each said goodbye and 15 years passed without her sending those pictures. I'd wish, over the years, that I could see them, but I decided that there were just things in life you have to accept. In 2017, I tried one more time. I wrote Clara's daughter an email and said I would never bother her again for the photos, but could she please put herself in my position. Could she imagine what it would be like to know someone had photos of you before you were four, photos you had never seen? If she could imagine what that was like, would she please send me copies? Within a few days she sent me, by email, seven photos that she thought were probably me.

One had my name on the back. Two were not me—the girl in the photos was too old. Three looked like they were me and two of them were iffy. It was wonderful, and a long time coming. Shortly after, she and I became Facebook friends. I like feeling a little connection to her. At least I know there is someone out there that knew Dorothy.

One of the biggest regrets in my life was that I didn't get in the car and drive to Delaware to meet with Clara and Walter *immediately* after getting back from meeting my family in Berlin back in 2000. I think

I would have gotten more answers, and the photos, and a chance to spend time with my former nanny and my godfather. It was too late. I was locked into my teaching contract, still taking care of my mother, and everything just seemed too busy and too complicated at the time. I should have sorted it out, made a list of my priorities, and followed through. But life has a way of doing what it wants.

One of the photos that Dorothy's granddaughter sent to me in 2017 – being held by my nurse, Clara.

With my first adoptive mother, Dorothy, and my nurse in Germany.

Chapter Thirty-Four

2000—Connecting Hearts

Ramona and Dieter both wrote back after they read my email to them. My heartfelt thoughts touched them.

First Ramona wrote:

"I read your mail twice and both times I had to cry. You said so lovely things and I wish I could use only half so good words in English to tell you how special you became to all of us and how much we love you. It is really hard to write beautiful things in English for me but I am sure you felt that we have these feelings you described in your letter in connection with you, too. That's why I had to cry, you just spoke out of my heart. My expression is not as good as yours but I am sure you know that what I am saying all comes from deep inside of my heart. And of course it was a pleasure for me to give up my room for you and to visit special places with you. I loved translating for you – I enjoyed every second together with you. I hope so much that it will not take so long time to meet you again."

Dieter wrote:

"Dear little sister, Jim and Ann! It was just three days ago when you flew home and I am already longing for you, for your laughter, cheerfulness and I want to hug you. Perhaps you don't know how much joy you brought into our

lives. Alas, only two weeks we spent together but these two weeks also changed our lives a bit…I have to tell you that I am very longing for you and our next meeting, and the waiting for it will be long and hard. Take care, that I don't mash you when I see you again. I always see your good and warm and friendly eyes in my mind and how you are always smiling like the sun. It was a wonderful time with you. I think that we will take Jim and Ann also to our heart when we meet them personally.

"We send all the best to you and yours and for you dear little sister I send an extra kiss. Stay as you are, this is how I love you. I remain as your big small brother, Dieter."

Klaus loved to write letters. He did not have a computer or an answering machine, but he did try to keep in touch. On Sept 18, 2000, while still in Berlin, he wrote: *"…thank you, thank you very much, for visiting us! Thank you for coming to Berlin. You have made our everyday life a lot richer, that's what I am thanking you for with all my heart. Even if my little jokes did not seem very humorous in front of our brothers, I could feel that you have a very good sense of humor. You have a very good heart, and that I know…You have seen into our soul, and you have found you and your inner being in us, just like we found us in your being. We will surely remember your visit for a long time, as if you were in Berlin right in the midst of us, your brothers and sister. How many years have to go by sometimes until people find each other? I hope with all my heart, dear Bonnie, that we meet again soon. Until then, all the best! Remember all of us like we will remember you, which is happy, uncomplicated, and humorous….One should not complain about fate, because God smoothes our way, but how nice would it have been, if we had gotten to know each other a few years earlier! But let us be happy, that even though late, we had a pretty good happy end! Thank you, our God! Until soon, dear Bonnie, your brother Klaus, who has taken you into his heart."*

In October of that year, Klaus again wrote a lovely letter.

"Dear Bonnie! I am back in Frankfurt and back to everyday life. Above all I want to thank you again for the wonderful presents, dear Bonnie. Irene (his common-law wife*) thanks you, too. She was very glad. She never thought of getting so nice presents from you. We will meet again one day healthy and*

*happy in La Crosse. That would be wonderful. I would learn how to swim in the Mississippi River and then jump into the Michigan Lake, to 'present' my sporty figure. What do you say, dear Bonnie? I assume that you are going to have to laugh hardily. Dear sister heart, please say hi to your husband Jimmy and your daughter Ann. On the pictures one only sees happy faces that could really make one jealous. I wish you a happy time in Wisconsin. See you later in La Crosse. (*He never made it to Wisconsin*). Your old and fat big brother from little Germany, Klaus (*64 at the time*)."*

As I said, Klaus loved to send letters. A few weeks later I got this:

"Dear Bonnie, Thank you very much for the nice letter with the terrific pictures....I am still thinking about all of us in Berlin. We should call each other someday. Now to Cowboy Jimmy: Is he being nice to you? Yes? He better be really nice to our little sister because if he isn't, I will swim overseas and he will be. But, if you don't have a reason to complain, then I will take off the swim vest, and you can say hi to him. Please also say hi to my niece, Ann. I am amazed about her versatile talents. Did she also inherit some of Cowboy Jimmy's genes? For example the horseback riding? It cannot be from our German genes since we don't even know how a riding horse looks like.

*We urban people catch a glimpse of a rabbit, a dog, or a cat at the most.... on my terrific Swiss Bicolor watch (*I gave it to him*) it is 8:15 pm. I will make myself a soup now and then I will go to the basement and get my beer, because a 'human' does not live with soup alone. Dear Bonnie, are your cassettes the same as ours? If so, I would record you one with German folk songs, like Loffel Polka, Bavarian Landler, and Schuhplattler music – typical Oktoberfest wind music, etc. Please let me know.... I see that I will never learn 'swimming' and am able to put the swim vest on the peg. Your fat old big brother, the first hippo in Germany with his own swim vest. Dear Bonnie, what would you like better as a brother, a fat big hippo, or a small seahorse? I don't want to be hard on your nerves, so that you can digest all calmly. I hope that Cowboy Jimmy doesn't shoot me, if I come, because I am frightened of the loud bang!"*

I missed them—all of them, even my sister the sourpuss. I had visions of us spending many years getting to know each other better. Life didn't go exactly as planned, but then, when does it ever? I learned this: It's best to enjoy what is happening in the present. Don't plan for the future because it's going to be what it's meant to be.

Chapter Thirty-Five

There's More to the Story

Despite the fact that we emailed so much info about each other before I arrived on German soil, and despite the fact that we talked late into each evening about anything and everything that we could think of to get to know each other, I still had some things I had not shared with them. One was about losing our first baby. I wanted them to know why the year 1977 was special to me. Our first baby died on the same day that he was born.

Both Gerhard and Anna died that same year, and yes, I guess it's true, *death comes in threes*. In writing to them about this, I said that I wished I had known that our baby had a grandfather and great-grandmother taking care of him in Heaven. We had named the baby Erik Michael. It was going to be Marcus Henry after my dad and Jim's dad, but when we realized that he was not going to live, we decided not to.

The name Erik Michael came to me *after* he was born, just out of the blue. If it had been a girl (something we didn't know ahead of time back in those days) she was to be named Erika. I wrote to Dieter:

Jim and I waited years to have children, and my folks were thrilled when I did because they were getting older and worried they would never see any grandchildren. My pregnancy proceeded fine for a while, but then it became obvious there was a problem. They started monitoring the baby (and me) every week. On February 28, 1977, they decided that the time had come, the baby was stressed, and they said they were going to do a c-section on me. The doctors decided the baby could not handle a natural delivery. Later, after he was born, I got to see him in an incubator. He was only 3 ½ pounds. They said I could hold him the following day. At 10:00 that night he died. Jim had to deal with everything, because I was not allowed out of the hospital because in those days you stayed in the hospital a week after a C-section. They did an autopsy and discovered that he was born without kidneys. Jim had to bury our baby without me...but his family and mine were there with him."

We did some genetic testing after that because we were worried about the same thing happening again. We were told that this disorder, Renal Agenesis, was more prevalent in baby boys, and that chances of it happening again to us were no greater than any other couple.

Two weeks after our son died my adoptive parents came to our house. They told us that my birth mother's name was Erika. *What a weird coincidence.* I never had a real birth certificate. Mary and Mark had told me I didn't have one. Apparently, I did have one. They gave it to me and there I was, 29 years old, seeing my birth certificate for the first time. I think it really blew their minds that I was considering Erika as a name and had called the baby Erik. Mary kept asking me how I came up with that name. I said, "I have no idea."

Years before, Mark had created a legal U.S. birth certificate for me. It allowed me to get a passport and a social security card when I was 18, and it allowed me to get married. I never questioned it and never realized there was another birth certificate.

Another coincidence with names: I was lucky enough to be pregnant again when the anniversary of Erik's death arrived. I was sure it was a girl because everything *felt* better. We wanted to name her Katherine. I thought that Katie or Kate would be good nicknames. Mary was furious. How could I possibly consider *that* name when her older sister, Catherine, lived in Florida with a man who was not her husband. It would be like honoring her for living *in sin. How could Mary hold her head up if any of her friends found out?* So, in true daughter of Mary Singer Spettel fashion, I gave up my name choice and then decided on Anna. Jim liked it but was afraid that kids would tease her and call her Anna Banana. We settled on Ann Elizabeth, but I called her Anna Banana just to tease Jim.

When I found my birth family I discovered that my grandmother on my mother's side was Anna, and she looked a lot like our Ann. I told Ann I would pay for her to change her name to Anna, but she said it would be too much work.

Our daughter, Ann.

It struck me right away how much my grandmother, Anna, looked like my daughter, Ann.

Chapter Thirty-Six

Half or Whole?

"To Whom It May Concern. I have found my birth family after 52 years. I had a wonderful journey to meet them, but we are not sure if we are full siblings. We know we have the same mother, but we are wondering if we have the same father. So, I would like us to get tested. My brother lives in Berlin, Germany and I live in Wisconsin, so how do we go about doing this and when do you want payment, etc? Thank you, Bonnie Willemssen"

On September 29, 2000, I received an answer to my query from the DNA Diagnostic Testing Center in Ohio. I was told that they could indeed provide testing for someone in Germany. They would send the kit directly to my brother with complete instructions for collecting the sample. It would have a prepaid return package for Dieter to ship samples directly back to the International U.S. Siblingship Study. For the person in the U.S. (me) "The scheduling department at their DNA center will coordinate an appointment for the tested party in the U.S. to go to a medical laboratory or hospital near their area. If you know for a fact that you and your sibling share the same biological mother or father, then you would have a full sibling test to determine if you share both biological parents."

Cost for a full sibling test, without tested parents included, was $875.00. Comparisons were generally $15–$45 per person (the additional cost was for collecting the samples). Testing time would take about 4–6 weeks once all samples arrived in the laboratory.

The center said the results would yield a "likelihood of a percentage." They said that usually they could achieve a probability of a percentage either in the 90% for inclusion or the lower teens range for an exclusion. "We cannot guarantee a certain percentage when performing a siblingship study because we do not know what the DNA patterns will reveal, but DNA is the most conclusive way to test for paternity and biological relationship."

Dieter and I had agreed that just the two of us would do the DNA testing. I said I would pay for all of it as I was the one that really wanted/needed to know if, when they talked about *their* father, they were talking about *my* father. The total cost was about $1000.00.

The kit arrived in Berlin. Dieter took care of things at his end, and I went to the hospital and did what I had to do at my end which was to go, alone, into a large room and fill out some papers. Then a notary-type person came in and asked me some questions and signed that I was who I said I was.

Then the lab technician came in and the notary person had to watch the blood be drawn and labeled. It felt very odd; like I was a prisoner being prepped for jail. Jim and I left the next day for Arizona. Although we were gone for only a few weeks, early results of the test were sent to Dieter and to me. The results were 99.5% that we were positively *full* brother and sister. He called Helga and told her, whereupon she called our phone in Wisconsin and left a message. When we got back from Arizona I listened to her message (all in German). She sounded so excited and happy, but I didn't understand what was going on. *What was she so happy about?* The next day Jim went to the post office to get the mail they had held for us. There was a letter from the DNA testing site stating the results. *Then I knew what Helga was so excited about.*

Dieter wrote:

"Hello little sister. Isn't it wonderful? We are full siblings yet. I got the DNA test report. We visited Aunt Sophie and chatted more than four hours about God and the world. She said she never gave Erika a promise to the death not to speak about the whole theme. This time Aunt said she remembers that Gerhard didn't know if he was your father and Erika thought you are the child of another man. She was alone for three years. The most important thing is that you know now who your father was. We (would be) glad even if we got another result. Therefore I had the feeling, when you've been here, that I have known you for my whole life, and we think right with 'the two left slippers.'"

By this time I had already found pictures of me that looked exactly like pictures of Gerhard, *our common father.* I paired them up, made photocopies for each of my siblings, and sent them off to Germany. The photos proved to me—and them—that Gerhard was my father. The DNA testing just made it official.

So, that question was answered. I had a birth father, and it was their father. We were full brothers and sisters. Every story they told me of their father was a story about my father. For good or bad, Gerhard Herman Paul was my father, too.

My birth parents.

Copy of the proof that we were
FULL brothers and sisters:

DNA Sibship Test Report

DNA DIAGNOSTICS CENTER

Report Date 12/21/2000

8804   27

Case 70763	Alleged Sibling A	Alleged Sibling B
Name	Bonnie A. Willemssen	Dietrich Paul
DoB - Race	7/30/48	4/16/39
Date Collected	10-25-00	11-18-00
Test No.	70763-20	70763-21

Interpretation	Combined Sibship Index **207.7210**	Probability of Sibship **99.5%**

My papa at 26, me in 6th grade.

Me at 23 years of age, and Papa

Dieter, 18 years old, and Me at 21

Papa, Me in holy communion veil.

Me and Dieter

Chapter Thirty-Seven

2000—Trying To Keep In Touch

Letters crossed the Atlantic. It was such a thrill when the mail came and there was something from Germany. I was beginning to accept the fact that I had a sister and three brothers. It was still amazing. I was no longer an only child; I was only *raised* as an only child. I no longer had just parents, I had *adoptive* parents and *birth* parents. Now I had to clarify whom I was speaking about when I spoke of family—there were three different sets. It was even confusing for me at times. I had to think of whom my audience was. If I was talking to someone who would never see me again then they didn't need to know my birth family story. Was I talking to someone who knew I was adopted? They would be thrilled to hear I found my birth family and might want to know the story. It's one of the reasons I'm writing this book. Naturally, my family and my friends are interested. I want to get it all out of my head and onto paper. I need to free up my brain cells for other endeavors.

Helga wrote to me in October.

"Dear Bonnie, I am thinking of you very often. If you are okay with that I would like to come in spring, by myself. Nobody has to take care of me. I am going to find my way by myself. Maybe April? Consider, I am already old and you never know how long I'll be living for. If you don't want it, please say so, and then I am going to Spain."

A letter (in German and translated by my neighbor) from Detti who had gone into the hospital with liver disease after my visit:

"Hello, dear Bonnie! I think you know from Dieter that I am still in the hospital. I feel better now but who knows. I lost 64 pounds. I am very thin in body and soul. No beer and no alcohol at all. I have to make a hard diet. Enough of me. Those few hours were very nice with you and the whole family. I can read the German you sent and if not, I will ask Dieter for the rest, what I don't know. The pictures with us all together show how glad we are to see you back after (such a) long time. My girlfriend with whom I have lived together for four years now comes every day to the hospital to visit me. Sometimes she brings Charlene along with her – our baby with four legs. The pleasure is always big. Not very long time till X-Mas, and if God wants so, I will be at home then. In the hope of hearing from you soon, dear Bonnie, I remain as your new brother, Detti,"

In November, Dieter wrote of the cold and winter coming to Berlin. He mentioned that Helga went to the travel agency and that she might want to stay for two weeks.

"I think every day of you, if you are walking barefoot over the cold (floors) in your cold country. Well, soon we will celebrate X-Mas. Eszter will fry a crispy X-Mas goose, we will decorate our Christmas tree and have a delicious X-Mas supper and relax a bit. Well, my left slipper, I am always thinking of you because I see my bracelet (the ID bracelet I sent him that said TWO LEFT SLIPPERS. I had one made for me too) a thousand times a day on my wrist."

More letters followed from Dieter. He turned out to be quite a good writer. I know that Ramona did a lot of translating, but Dieter used the electronic translator that I left with him when I returned to the U.S. He was so thrilled to be able to work with it. He told me that he was always trying to learn English. In 1966 he completely translated a Jack London short story. He talked of putting the garden to bed at their weekend house, of life in Berlin, of putting pine on the graves at the cemetery.

Klaus wrote and thanked me for the gifts I sent.

In English he said, *"I dream of flying to Wisconsin sometime in the future. I hope Cowboy Jimmy will forget my jokes in the letter and don't shoot me when I come to La Crosse, but I cannot swim so many miles over the ocean! I* learned how in school, but that was 50 years ago and I forgot. I will write the rest in German. I've been working on this letter for two hours and only had breakfast today; now my tummy makes noises singing the "foodsong" and you can probably imagine what that means. Snarl, snarl, snarl. Well, I have to come to an end."

Ramona wrote in December of 2000 that she would be on vacation from the University (Humboldt) and not have access to a computer. We agreed to talk on the phone on December 24th. I told her Jim, Ann, and I would be leaving for Arizona after the holiday to stay with Jim's brother, David, in Tucson and to see how our new house was coming along in Green Valley. I would not have a computer either.

Ramona wrote:

"About Helga. Please don't worry so much about her and don't let her smoke in the house, she will smoke a lot more. I wouldn't give her much beer, only as much as she can handle and don't worry if she sometimes seems a bit scary. That is how she is sometimes and it is hard to handle even for us and we have known her for a long time. We all wish you Merry X-Mas and a good start into the New Year."

My annual Christmas letter that year was a joy to write.

"Dear Family and Friends, I cannot believe what an incredible year 2000 has been. So many things have happened and all of them have been wonderful. We bought property in Green Valley, AZ and will be building a vacation house soon. In April I got a phone call from my BROTHER. For those of you that know me well, you know that I was adopted, and that I was born in Berlin, Germany. Well, when I turned 50, Ann encouraged me to find my birth family. I hired a search consultant who discovered my birth mother and father had passed away, but that I had three brothers and a sister still living in Germany. What a shock! Needless to say, that was the most incredible phone call I have ever received."

The letter goes on to describe other things that happened that year—trips we took and what Ann was doing. But, of course, mostly people were excited about my journey of discovery and many emailed their congratulations.

On December 25th, Dieter wrote a note and said that his dreams had come true. They had 5.9 inches of snow and he was getting a white Christmas. He was thrilled. I was thrilled for him. I loved a white Christmas, also. He said they had gone to midnight Mass at the Protestant church. On the 26th—Boxing Day—they were going to eat "Bugs Bunny" as they did at Easter. He said Helga would be at his house the next day and that I could call between 3 o'clock and 4 o'clock our time. He wished us a nice trip to Arizona and a Happy New Year. "If it is possible, write an e-mail from there, but don't stress about it. Love to you all from the 3 Berliners. Your other left slipper, Dieter."

Also at Christmas of 2000, I had a neighbor translate my Christmas letter so I could send it to my German family. Part of what I wrote said, *"I wanted you to know that I love you and care about you and hope that we all have a long time to get to know each other better. I think that it will be a slow process with the distance between us, but someday it will be better. Jim and I will possibly come to Germany next summer if the political situation is okay. I can't wait to see you all."*

It ended up we did not go to Germany until 2003.

Chapter Thirty-Eight

2001—A Year Passes

In January I got a shock. Helga wrote and said she had her airline tickets and she would be coming on April 20th of 2001 and *leaving on May 9th. What?* I had worried about spending *two* weeks with her—now it was *three*. She said, "As you know, I drink beer and smoke. If I don't have that, I won't really feel well. I don't want to do a detoxication at your house. I only want to see how you live and how you are doing. I don't really like to go out to eat. I could make salads and cakes. Other than that, we will wait and see. Your sister, Helga." *Good grief. She didn't want to go out to eat. That was the staple of my life—eating out.*

Klaus wrote in February thanking me for a letter I had sent with pictures of our new house in Arizona and the view from the backyard. He told me he had informed his son Gerald in Utah of the existence of his "new joined aunt" and that he had given him my email address. He talked about Gerald's children:

"Bronte Mary is a great girl, 9 years old and my little sugar girl, Michaela, 4 years old. I will come to an end now. It does not matter how many words I write but only what they mean. Stay happy and healthy, until later. I am looking forward to coming to La Crosse and to see Gerald and Sue with the children. You can imagine how that is when you see your 'emigrated' child after

years. We will probably cry a lot. PS. I enclosed a little picture in the letter because I became even more beautiful and I did not want to keep that back from you! Love, the big Klaus."

Dieter often tried to fill me in on family relationships. He talked of his memories of our grandpa on Papa's side. First Papa's mother died in 1919 when he was 14 years old. Grandpa Hermann Paul (who was a tailor all his life), died from cancer in 1942. Dieter remembered that Grandpa Hermann would furtively give him candies and tell him not to tell Grandma. And Grandma Biesdorf (the 2nd wife) gave Dieter candies, too, and he wasn't supposed to tell Grandpa about it. "The grandmother on my mother's side was called *Oma* Tegel because she lived in the Tegel section of Berlin."

Dieter knew her very well and "...she was a wonderful, warm-hearted woman. Her whole life she gave all she had to her child and grandchildren. But she was so dominant. She couldn't tolerate a man on her side. She was a tailor, too, and the last years of her job she was the leader. The father of Erika was called *Appelopa* (apple-grandpa). They had a fruit stand in the covered market at Alexanderplatz. After he divorced Anna Jahnke (*Oma* Tegal) he married *Appeloma* (Frieda Mueller). She died in 1993 at the age of 93 years old."

Dieter said they didn't travel much when he was young; sometimes a day trip to a lake or a beach near Berlin. Nearly every year they were sent to a children's holiday camp of Gerhard's company, the VEB Taxi Berlin. Gerhard was a taxi driver his whole life, and most of his work was the night shift.

Dieter took his first vacation alone in 1955 to the Baltic Sea for three weeks. That was when he was in training for his first job—a sheet metal locksmith for *"air-conditions."* In 1967 Dieter was retrained to be an aircraft mechanic. He traveled every year somewhere; Poland, Prague, Moscow, and Budapest, either by train or plane. After the "downfall of the Wall of Shame" in 1989 they could travel all over the world. From the time Ramona was three months old the family flew to Budapest to visit Eszter's relatives three or four times a year. They often "made holidays" sponsored by the airline company to the Baltic Sea, to the German mountains, or to a health resort in Czechoslovakia.

Ramona wrote to reassure me that Helga's visit should be just fine if I just continued with our routine, and Helga would just have to fit in. *"If you have big problems in communication, what I don't believe, because you have hands and feet to talk with, if you have problems you can write it to me or she can type it and I will try to translate. But don't stress about it."*

In reality, it was much worse than I anticipated. I wrote and asked Ramona to ask Helga some questions about her habits. Here are Ramona's answers.

"She is sleeping till 8 or 9 but she will stand up earlier if it is necessary. She likes to go shopping but she can't walk a long time because her feet hurt. She doesn't want to go into a casino for gambling. She will eat everything you cook but she is not a big fish-fan. If there are some 'smoking allowed' restaurants she will go there with you. If there is a possibility to rent some movies it would be nice but not necessary. She will take something to read and some crosswords along. She will go to church with you. Also, she said she will eat whatever you make for her. She has only the German measures for her recipes, but I told her you would figure out a way to translate into American measures. What does 'earn her keep' mean?" (I had written that Helga could 'earn her keep' by cooking.)

Ramona told Helga to bring a swimsuit when she came to visit, as we had a hot tub she might want to get into. She also told her to bring some recipes if she wanted to do any cooking. Dieter wrote and told me she said she "didn't need any recipes because she is cooking from inside out."

April 12, 2001, I received another letter from Detti thanking me for the birthday card and money I sent to him. He still wrote "Bonny" instead of "Bonnie," but at least he wrote to me. He said his health was "like the weather in April, today rain, and tomorrow sunshine." He was out of the hospital and able to ride his bike again and walk his dog, Charly.

He went on to reassure me that he had not had a drop of alcohol "nor wine, beer, schnapps, champagne." He said he did not want to go back to the hospital, so he was trying to "live with the conscience of still being alive." He said Mama would always say "lived well and fast but a few years less." Detti did very well financially in DDR (during the Russian occupation) times.

"I was no communist, but we did not have unemployed people and everybody was socially secure. For my big apartment (three rooms, kitchen, bathroom, and balcony) I paid 78 Marks. Today, 700 Marks. I had a yard and 600 meters of land. Because of my sickness I had to sell. (Alcoholism?) *I hope this letter with a few pieces of information could contribute to our understanding of each other, since two worlds did separate us. To have a small big sister all of a sudden is almost unbelievable, how life goes. Even though we speak different languages, sometimes the heart speaks. Blood is thicker than water. For you, dear Bonny, and your family all the best and health from all my heart, your brother, Detti."*

I got an odd, very sad letter from Klaus in December. He seemed to want me to know about his previous life. He wrote:

"I was so surprised to hear about your existence. All these years without knowing about a second sister that wasn't with us. You were kept a secret. I cannot write my life history right now, but I'll give you a little resume. From the era of 1936 until 1947 I was a happy, uncomplaining kid. The time was nice, if also turbulent. Twice we were evacuated to Thuringen until 1945. But then, our father in 1947 came home from the prison camp and then my happy childhood is gone. Then I was beaten a lot and didn't know why. No loving words, no love, no trust, only strict rules. In 1954, when I was 17, since Papa was the way he was, I went over the border illegally to West Berlin.

I never went back to my parents' house. I never had a nice life. It was only a struggle for existence which I lost. I tried several experiences but most were bad. This year I will be 64. I am an old, sick man who is nothing and has nothing. I think, when I now look it over that I would have gladly exchanged places with you, but everybody has their own fate. How I have fought and struggled but everything didn't work out. Dear sister, I send you a couple pictures. Later, you will get more, just like you sent me."

I really didn't care anymore if some of them were odd (like Detti), uneducated (like Klaus), or distant (like Helga). They were all wonderful and interesting to me. They were my family and, for all their quirks, there was Dieter—my wonderful, smart, loving brother to counteract them. He was the cherry on top of the ice cream sundae.

Chapter Thirty–Nine

Long Lost Nephew

It was Saturday, March 24, 2001. I sat at my computer to catch up after having been in Arizona for three weeks. I saw an email that had come in on March 13th with the subject line LONG LOST NEPHEW? *What in the world was this about? Was it spam? Or a scam?*

"Bonnie, where to begin? I have been in contact with Klaus and Irene for a few years now. I received a letter from Klaus yesterday explaining that he had discovered that he had a sister, YOU! He sent me your email address/ phone number etc. and suggested that I write to you." It was signed Gerald Bringhurst.

My "new" nephew went on to tell me a bit about his life. He had two degrees, one in electronic engineering and one in computer software. I think it's amazing how successful someone can become despite their birth circumstances. His father, Klaus, barely finished high school, if he even did. Gerald's adoptive dad was in the army. He and his wife adopted Gerald in Germany, but he grew up in the United States. Gerald was married with two daughters, Bronte' and Michaela. He'd had contact with his birth father for the first time in 1985 when Gerald and his wife, Sue, were married. Over the years they had phone calls and letters going back and forth. Several times my nephew and his wife were able to meet with

Erhard, one of his three brothers on the east coast. Klaus had three sons with Irene—Gerald, Erhard, and Dieter.

Gerald asked me what Klaus' last name was. He didn't even know that. He was as much in the dark as I was, it seemed. Or perhaps I knew even a bit more. He asked if I had any email addresses for Klaus or the brothers, but I didn't. I barely knew what he was talking about at all. I did know that Klaus was an odd duck and it would never occur to him to provide all the necessary information such as a last name, and I knew he did not have a computer. Klaus didn't tell me anything about his family except once, when we were in Berlin, saying something about a son in Utah. I didn't question him about it at the time because I didn't know what he was talking about.

Following this first email from my new nephew was another one dated a couple days later. I felt so bad because we had been out of town and I had not seen these two emails right away. Poor Gerald must have wondered why his "new aunt" had not answered him. I immediately wrote and explained we had been out of town and that yes, he had reached the right person, but I needed time to answer him properly and would have to wait until later that day. I'm sure he was anxious to hear what I might be able to tell him.

A day later I wrote.

"Dear Gerald....shall I start by telling you that Klaus' last name is Paul? He and your mother never married but have been together for over 30 years. If you do not have any pictures of them I have plenty I can copy and send to you....I have also been adopted so I know that it's so hard to wait once you find a link to your past."

I then went on to tell him all about my quest to find my family. How I met them, the letters and phone calls, the pictures, and the DNA testing. I also asked him many questions about his life and family in Utah.

His return email said that his whole family was learning German for their upcoming trip to Germany. I wrote and asked if he knew if Klaus would be visiting him and perhaps us? Klaus told me many times he wanted to come to America and see us, although I could not imagine for one minute how he would manage on the airplane for all those hours sitting and not moving. And now, 18 years later, I can tell you that Klaus never got to America. Money was a big factor in his diminished lifestyle, and Klaus' eyesight was bad. He had cataract problems that could have been fixed, but he was afraid of the pain. He finally went through with the surgery when he could see nothing and could not ride his bike to the corner market any longer.

In August of 2001, Gerald's family went to a wedding in London. After that, they flew to Germany to meet his birth mother, Irene, and his father, Klaus, and his brother, Dieter (named after Klaus' brother). He said it was a great experience—that his birth mother was a great cook and that they were treated like "royalty."

Ann graduated from U of C Berkeley with a degree in Public Policy. We drove to California to help her move and on the way back to Wisconsin we stopped to meet my nephew and his family. They lived in Salt Lake City and we were invited for Sunday dinner. We parked our car and as I got out and started for the front door, Gerald came out to greet us.

The moment I saw him it took my breath away because he had my face. Of all the sibling and relatives I had met since 2000, he was the one who most looked like me. Poor guy. And it was such a nice visit. He and his wife and daughters were so gracious. The girls were beautiful and Sue their mother was funny and fun. It was a great time and I knew I wanted to see them again. But, has that happened? No, unfortunately it has not. With no reason to drive to northern California again, we have not traveled that way again. They have been busy with family and work and have not been able to visit us either. We keep in contact by email and Christmas cards and Facebook. How does it happen that the greatest things happen and we are sure we'll keep in contact forever, and then things fade?

Chapter Forty

2001—Helga's Trip

We drove to Minneapolis (two and a half hours away) to get Helga. Jim and I sat in an area where we could see people departing overseas flights and through customs. We watched her walk from the second-floor arrival area through a long corridor and to the first floor. As soon as she noticed us she started to wave and grin. Then she would walk a little farther before turning, waving, and grinning. It seemed like odd behavior, as she was not very exuberant when I had been with her before. Once we physically hugged, and she had met Jim, I helped her with her luggage while Jim went to get the car.

She wanted to get out to the street in the worst way. She *needed* a cigarette. Being an ex-smoker, I understood. While we waited for Jim to get the car, she pulled her shirt off her shoulder to show me that she was wearing a nicotine patch. She was very relieved to light up. I wondered about smoking while wearing the patch, but that was beyond my capabilities of translation.

I told her to tell me when she needed to stop to smoke. And she did, often. Already my translating skills were being put to the test; pointing out sights and reading the menu when we stopped to eat. I've never been good with long silences, so I kept trying to fill in the voids in the conversation. Poor Jim just drove the car.

The guest bedroom in our house in Wisconsin was in the basement. It was nice but had no windows or natural light. There was a private bathroom attached to the bedroom and I'm sure that Helga thought it was heaven. She also had access to the downstairs refrigerator (which was fully stocked with beer, thanks to Jim). There was a family room area with a TV and VCR player. I had gone to a local video store and rented about 15 movies they had that were in German. Ramona told me weeks later, after Helga returned to Berlin, that some of them were X-rated.

Because I felt that I did poorly with my German, I hired a gal named Miriam who was an exchange student from Hamburg attending the university for a year. She was sweet and smart and luckily when Helga met her she liked her, too. I had Miriam come to the house for dinner or go out to dinner with us as often as her schedule allowed. I would ask her to ask Helga questions. I did learn a few things about Mama, Papa, and life in Germany, but Helga was very private and not willingly forthcoming.

I took Helga to meet my mother. Mary was in the nursing home and pretty much in a world of her own. She was happy, but not aware of who people were. She was always glad to see my face but called me different names—mostly her sisters' names. That was okay. I was glad she was content. They loved her at the home. For some strange reason, she had become the proverbial "sweet little old lady." They had no idea what a force to be reckoned with she had been in her former life.

When I took Helga into my mother's room and told her who Helga was, Mother started to cry. I was shocked by her reaction. Helga interpreted it as acknowledging that we were sisters. She hugged and thanked Mother in German for taking care of me. It was very bizarre—I really didn't think my mother was capable of understanding much of what was happening around her. I wasn't sure how to handle my mother's reaction, having just expected her to glance over and then look away. I was kind of shaken by the experience, but Helga, not realizing how unusual this encounter was, seemed happy to have been introduced to my adoptive mother.

I could hardly breathe for those three weeks that Helga was with us. I'm ashamed to say I just wanted her visit to be over. It was wonderful to know I had a sister, and even to have her visit, but three weeks was way too long.

She smoked outside on the patio. I let her help me with some of the gardening. Mostly she was happy just sitting and smoking and drinking. When the weather was bad, or it was dark, Jim had set up a chair and a table and an ashtray in the garage so she could smoke, and she made her way up those basement steps a whole lot of times, bad feet notwithstanding.

I counted the days. To get away from her I pretended I had meetings or work-related things just so I could leave the house. She pretty much left Jim alone and he didn't pay much attention to her unless she said, "Jim, beer!" Then he knew the refrigerator in the basement was empty. One time we took her with us to the grocery store and let her pick out her own beer. She picked out a couple of *cases* and chose several cartons of cigarettes that lasted her a only a few days. I took her shopping for good athletic shoes because she was so interested in mine when I was in Germany. I bought her a nice pair and she loved them. They felt so good on her feet that she wore them back home to Germany on the plane.

I was feeling guilty about not bonding with her like I did with Eszter, so I had a big party while she was there. I wanted my family and friends to meet my new sister. She helped me with the fixings and must have wondered about the huge amount of food I was preparing. I had Miriam come to help translate. When I sent the invitation, I put a German phrase with phonetic pronunciation in each invite and asked everyone to repeat it to Helga when they met her.

I don't think Helga liked the party too much. She and Miriam sat on the patio and Helga smoked. My best friend, Mary, spent a lot of time with Helga. Mary and I, friends since we were four, were "sisters in spirit," and she was so happy to meet my biological sister. Mary has an excellent memory and was able to chat with Helga quite well in German, remembering phrases from her high school German.

I had other dinners at our house—with people that might make Helga feel comfortable. Our next door neighbors enjoyed meeting her and she them. I had friends from Germany over. Each time we had an event, Miriam was present. We went a couple of times to Jim's sister Karen's and her partner Betty's house to sit in front of their big outdoor fire pit. We chatted, sang, and roasted marshmallows. Jim's dad, Hank, was present at every occasion and I think that Helga was interested in marrying him. She wanted to know all about him. Was he married? Was he lonely? Did he want to get married again?

It was kind of weird. I told her he liked her but that he was not interested in getting married again. That stopped that line of thought. I think she envisioned living right there in La Crosse with all of us. *That would have been an interesting turn of events.*

Before she left she handed me some clothes and asked if she could leave them at our house for her next trip. *Next trip?! Oh, Lord!* Of course, I told her she could. But then I said, in German, next time it cannot be quite as long, only two weeks. *What was I saying? I would have preferred one week.* And I told her I could not pay for her ticket next time. *Yes, I paid for her plane ticket, but I didn't want to start a precedent.*

I was ready for her visit to end. We still had to get her to the Minneapolis airport—several more hours of forced captivity in the car. At this point I was barely making an attempt to chat or keep her entertained. I don't know what she did most days, but she must have thought I was a mighty busy person as I was "running off" for part of each day. We left early for Minneapolis because I thought she'd like to see Mall of America. But, we had no more walked through one entrance of the mall then she made a mad dash for the next exit to light up a cigarette. I realized it was a waste of time to show her around the mall. She was clearly not interested. We went somewhere for lunch and were still hours early for her flight because of the aborted mall trip.

So, there we sat waiting for time to pass. Tornados were sighted in the area, and the weather began to get very bad. I said to Jim, "Dear God, what if the flight is canceled and we have to take her to a hotel tonight?" But, a stroke of luck happened, the airlines announced that because everyone was checked in for that overseas flight, they were going to start boarding and fly out early.

Hurray! We got Helga to the proper place. I explained what was going on. I told her that the weather was looking really bad and we'd like to get on the road so we could get home. It was 4 o'clock and she could see out the window that the sky was not looking great. I went up to the airline desk and explained that I had a passenger who did not speak English, and could they make sure she got on the plane. I went back and explained the situation to Helga as best I could, hugged her, and when I was out of sight, I practically *ran* out of that building. In fact, we were chased by tornados all the way home. I knew then and there that I was not going to invite her to come back again.

Dieter wrote to me in June saying that Helga "very liked her trip and especially she went into raptures about the nature around your house, and she said that all the people were very friendly to her." *I was glad that she seemed happy about her trip.*

Helga's THREE WEEK visit

Hegla's favorite place – on our patio
smoking a cigarette and drinking a beer.

Chapter Forty–One

2001—Ramona's Visit

After Ann graduated from Oberlin College in the spring of 2001, she moved to Minneapolis to start her career. Her first position blended her two degrees, Finance and Dance. She became the Managing Director of the business end of Zenon Dance School. We were so happy to have her so close to home. We never expected her to move again and certainly didn't love that it ended up being so far away—California—but she spent three years in Minneapolis.

In the summer we prepared for Ramona's visit. She would stay for five weeks and we would pretend that she had an internship at Jim's store. She would arrive on July 18, 2001. I was so excited to have her visit. Most importantly, she would meet her first cousin and I hoped they would bond like sisters.

Our emails to each other included questions about our diet, "What about your diet, dear *Tante* Bonnie?" We discussed the weather in Wisconsin in July. I offered her slippers and t-shirts and sweatshirts of Ann's so she could put other things in her suitcases. She was flying standby, so exact times for her to fly into Chicago would be up in the air. She would fly Lufthansa because that was the company her dad worked for. She could fly for free, but Lufthansa only flew into Chicago. We would need to drive 5 hours to get her and 5 hours to drive her back to La Crosse.

"Hello Dears! Happy Whitsun. *It is a holiday here called Whit Monday. I am excited to meet you again Bonnie, and to meet Jim and Ann personally. We were just talking and writing and I am very curious, how they are in real life. I am eager to see where you live; of course I have seen everything on pictures. I hope you don't make too much trouble in your habits. I don't want to disturb or bother you, please live your life as usual, when I am there. I hope you will not have so many problems with me as with Helga concerning the conversation, at least I can speak a bit of English."*

I was so excited to see her. I was worried I wouldn't remember what she looked like. But, who could forget a pretty girl with a wild mountain of blond kinky hair? She arrived. Smiles! Hugs! Joy! We got her luggage and off we went for the long ride home back to La Crosse.

"Hello Eszter and Dieter, Ramona is being a very good girl. We are having a good time. We are trying to do lots of interesting things. This weekend she will spend with Ann. It will be great for them to get to know each other. We are having nice hot weather now and Ramona loves it but it is humid so we have had to turn on the air conditioning which she does not like too well. I think she will be trying to bring Augie, one of our cats, back to Germany with her. Augie has fallen in love with her, too."

We tried to do a lot of different things with Ramona. We drove to Minneapolis twice. One time was the first week after she arrived so she could meet Ann. Ann was working, but we met for lunch. Later we met Ann again for dinner. I picked a Japanese restaurant thinking that Ramona would find that interesting, but it turned out to be a poor choice because of the noise level. A week later I took her up again to stay with Ann in her apartment.

The next week, we took her to Wisconsin Dells. We met Ann there and spent the day at Noah's Ark Water Park. Unfortunately, the weather was bad, so we left the park early. We played miniature golf at one of the "Goofy Golf" sites in the Dells, but it was still too cold to enjoy ourselves. Poor Ramona, all she wanted was hot weather and it was an unusually cold July. Later we ate at a pizza place. Unfortunately, Ramona did not warm up till we turned on the heat in the car.

We spent time with various relatives while Ramona was with us. She especially liked going to Karen and Betty's house because they always had a huge outdoor fire burning. That is something Ramona and Dieter and Eszter did at their garden house in Germany, and they loved that kind of activity—sitting around the fire, telling stories, and expounding on life in general. We also took a day trip to Lanesboro, MN to go biking. Ramona used Ann's bike and she enjoyed the cute little town with its wonderful, paved biking trails.

On August 7th I got an email from my brother. He was looking into how many passengers would be on board certain Lufthansa flights so we could plan when to take Ramona back to Chicago to fly home.

"Hope you are well and our Mokush (Dieter's pet name for his daughter) does not trouble you on account because of her long stay at you. Until now she spent only 14 days a few times in the U.S.A. but now she will learn very much of English and she can better study the mentality of Americans. We wish you more nice days together. Alas, Heaven knows when we will meet again. All the best to you and yours. Your big brother the other left slipper. Dieter."

The five weeks went fast and soon we were taking Ramona back to Chicago to return to Berlin. Unlike when Helga flew home, I was sad to see Ramona go. She fit right into our home and our lives.

On August 22nd, Ramona wrote to thank us for her experiences.

"Dear Tante *Bonnie and* Onkel *Jim! A special thank you to Jim for the time you spent to search for a place for an internship and to write this paper for me so I have a proof to show my boss. ALSO, I want to thank you that you took me to nearly all restaurants in La Crosse and in Minneapolis and so my shape is ruined forever. Also, I enjoyed my trip to Minneapolis, it was so good to meet Ann finally and I really liked her. I hope you get back to normal life again and I apologize that I stole so much of your time. I very enjoyed my trip and I wasn't bored at all. There was always something to do; biking, walking, watching TV, studying, eating, sightseeing, shopping and meeting new people. I was glad to meet so many of your friends; it was always interesting for me to*

see how people live, what they think about Germany a.s.o. Love and greetings to you all. Ramona."

Ramona spent many weeks with us. Met her cousin. Absorbed a little of the American way of life. What did her heart feel about the difference in their upbringings?

At this time, Jim's dad was a very healthy 89 and riding his bike five miles a day. We still spent Thanksgiving and Christmas in La Crosse with Ann coming home for both holidays. My sister went to Spain that season and Dieter and his family spent Christmas at home. I spoke to Klaus on the phone on Christmas Eve.

It had become normal to refer to "my brothers" and "my sister" and not have my mind question my words. We were a family. I had found a family. A big family. It was wonderful to have siblings. As I look back, I didn't really hate being an only child. It was what it was. I guess if anything, I wished I had a sibling to be my ally at all stages of my life. But, I'm sure each only child feels that way. I also would have loved to have a sibling when my folks were getting on in years and needed my help so much. It was unfortunate that Ann was still young when they were old. I had a hard time dividing my time, and I know everyone suffered for that.

Chapter Forty–Two

2001—Cabin Fever

Dieter had travel fever. They went to so many places—to Florida after I had visited, to the Caribbean in March. Anytime there was an opportunity to be somewhere warm they took it. Flying cheap was such an advantage for them. Jim and I were headed to Arizona to spend a couple weeks in our new house. Mary was in a nursing home and many times I thought the end was near, but she was a tough old bird and always rallied. The nurses said that she thrived because of my care and diligent efforts on her behalf. I was there almost every day to visit her, and would have relatives visit if I was out of town. I wanted to meet my Maker and be able to say that I had taken care of her despite some rocky times in our relationship.

In October of 2001, Mary passed away at the age of 98. She had a good life, and I cried. Despite her lifelong paranoia and her need to run everyone's life, she was someone who really tried to do the right thing. I know she wanted to do right by me; she just wasn't able to rise above her mental issues. I was sad to see her depart from my world, but most of the sadness was because of our inability for us to ever really bond.

This is the letter I wrote one year after having been to Germany to meet my family: September 2001: *"Dear Helga, Klaus, Dieter, and Detti, this is your younger sister writing to you in English and hoping that Ramona will translate into German. It has been over a year since we learned of each other's existence. I know you are all happy to have had me find you, but I want to tell you what it has meant to me. Always I hoped that I had a family somewhere in Germany that was waiting for me to "come home." I used to imagine (when I was young) that my big brother would come to the door one day, ring the doorbell, and tell my parents that he had been searching for me and finally found me, and had come to take me home. I didn't always get along well with my adoptive parents, especially my mother, so that was a fond dream of mine…to be found by my REAL family.*

"As time went on and I knew you were probably all behind the Iron Curtain, it seemed impossible to look for you. I gave up even thinking about a family in Germany. When The Wall came down in '89 I thought about searching, but at that time I was busy dealing with my adoptive father's dementia and my adoptive mother's declining health. I so regret finding you so late in our lives. A big regret is that Mama didn't know I grew up relatively happy and healthy. She must have wondered about me over the years. My second regret is that Papa didn't know that I was his child. The third regret is that we didn't get to be part of each other's lives earlier so we could know each other better. My fourth regret is that Ann and Ramona, who are so close in age, couldn't have known each other when they were younger. I wish I could have been at the kitchen table with you to hear all Mama's and Papa's stories of when they were young. The pictures you have shared with me have been precious, and they mean more than I can ever say. So, although those are my regrets, I know that nothing can be changed—we will go forward from here. I am just so grateful that we have found each other NOW and that we are all still alive.

"I will never forget, for as long as I live, the thrill of having Dieter (and Helga) call me on that early morning in April. I expected perhaps a polite letter telling me some health information and probably saying that you were not sure who my father was. Your enthusiastic response was so unexpected. When Dieter told me that he had searched for me I was totally overwhelmed that my brother had been looking for me. Just to know that he had wanted to find me changed something inside of me in that moment. MY BIRTH FAMILY HAD WANTED TO FIND ME!!

When I actually stood next to you (in the airport) I felt that I was not a part of my body, but that I was looking down from the ceiling at all of us meeting and being in the same room. I stood with five total strangers who also happened to be my sister, my three brothers, and my niece. The trip for me was a dream comes true. At 52, I had found my family. Such a wonderful thing to know that the little hole in my heart is filled up now, and what a thrill to see parts of me in each of you.

So, what does the future hold for us? I hope that each of you would sit and write down memories from your growing up years. I love you all. I pray that we have long, happy, healthy lives so that we can continue to get to know each other better and be a part of each other's lives. Love and good wishes from your little sister, Gerda."

Right after my letter was sent, the tragedy of 9/11 happened in New York City. This was the email Ramona wrote.

"Dear Bonnie, dear Jim, we are full of consternation about the awful tragedy that happened in New York and Washington DC. I was totally confused when I was turning on the TV last night. I wasn't able to move and it took some time till I could tell Mum and Dad what happened. What people are these who can do such terrible things? We are so glad that you don't live nearby one of those cities and hopefully you are okay except of the shock which we got all, but as we can see, you are never safe anywhere. The whole world is in mourning with the American nation and we as a family could understand your feelings especially. Hopefully there will not start another world war after this occurrence."

Dieter wrote to me about ten days later.

"Dear little sister! This day I answer your lovely letter you send to all of us. Reading your lines now I can't read further on because I must cry, poor little sister, it must have been an anguish for you, the feeling, that your real parents expelled you and your yearning for your right family. Then the questions: Have I got any brothers and sisters? Would they like to have me nearby? Did they grown up happy? Are they well? But, in order to compensate for your anguish, you could grow up in a free country without financially problems.

There was only the question of the little girl: When will my big brother come to take me along to my real family? Me for my part, I can affirm that I sincerely love you from brother to sister. I was ever so pleased about meeting you, although we found us just in our late years of our life. I also see it a bit like to make up for the anguish you had because your (birth) parents do not have the possibility to make up anymore. Well, in addition to that I felt subconsciously that you are somewhere for my whole lifetime. It was like an invisible line to you. Maybe I heard talk between our parents about you… perhaps they spoke about your stay in the U.S. and I don't now know. Perhaps I have forgotten it or repressed it. When I was young I stole an English book from Helga and read it at night hidden under the blanket with a little flashlight. I read and wrote my first English sentences and there was always my dream of America and it seemed to me to be paradise. I wanted to go there at any price but then life brought other things to me."

By the time Dieter got into school, English lessons were forbidden. He tried later to take some English classes, but ended up being forced to do his lessons only in Russian. *"During the time of the GDR, all English and American things were frowned upon and America was enemy number one for the idiots which governed our country."*

In 1967 Dieter met a man from California who was traveling through East Germany. They met in a *Brewhaus*. They exchanged addresses and corresponded a number of times after that. When the Wall of Shame came down, visiting this "friend" was the first thing that Dieter and his family did. "My dream came true; finally I went to the U.S.A."

In the late 60s there were English classes offered. Dieter took English one night and another night Hungarian.

"When Helga first called and said we have a sister in America, my heart jumped for joy. I was so happy. I have a little sister in America and she reported and announced herself. Sorry I ringed you out of bed so early that morning at April 27th, but it was worth it, we could not lose more time. The culmination of all and the greatest joy was to receive you here and to take you into our hearts. During your stay here, I found more and more out that we are so much in common, which can only be sister and brother with the same blood. We love you from the bottom of our hearts and we do not want you ever will go out of our hearts. As you said in your lines, the past is over, we have to see forward and we should from our relations and connections, we cannot change the past. Only God knows how much time we have left to enjoy our brothers' and sister's love.

*Now I know there was a reason about my whole lifetime longing to American.
I felt in my subconscious that you have been there somewhere."*

In January of 2002, the two cats took their first long car trip to
Arizona. One loved it and the other threw up constantly. I continued to
teach and work with student teachers at the university. Jim would spend
time in Green Valley and I would fly back and forth when I could.

Chapter Forty-Three

2002–2003 The Passing Years

In the summer of 2002, Dieter, Eszter, and Ramona all flew into Chicago where we picked them up and brought them back to La Crosse. Our house had a full basement with a large bedroom and a good-sized bathroom and a fairly comfortable couch for Ramona to sleep on. There was a TV and a refrigerator down there, but it was a basement—with no windows. But, it seemed to be a pretty good place to lay their heads at the end of the day.

The hardest part of their visit happening at that time was that I had been diagnosed with Valley Fever a month before. It's a fungal infection that people contract in southern Arizona that goes into your lungs, among other places, and leaves you feverish, achy, and *extremely* tired. Cleaning the house and getting ready to entertain was not easy. And once my family was there, it was hard to try to keep up with the cooking and cleaning and entertaining. I'm one of those people that likes to be the "hostess with the mostess" so it was not in my nature to sit back and let guests fend for themselves. On top of that, I did not tell them ahead of time that I had gotten sick because I didn't want them to cancel this long anticipated and already planned and paid for trip. I kept telling myself that I would be fine when they came. It worked out, mostly because I agreed, after Jim forced me, to cut back on my "duties" and let everyone help out.

We wanted them to see as much of the countryside as we could. Dieter, who loved to fish, got several experiences to do that. Friends of ours, Jim and Bette Michaels, let us use their cottage on the Mississippi for a day so Dieter could fish, take the boat out, and enjoy a day on the water. And he loved it. Jim's dad, Hank, also joined us. Fishing all day was right up his alley.

We all went bike riding on the paved bike trails of Minnesota. We enjoyed campfires and cooking over an open fire at Jim's sister Karen's (and her partner, Betty's) house in the woods. Dieter was in 7th Heaven. We sang, told stories, roasted marshmallows, and made s'mores. My cousin, Ray Opitz and his wife Sharon, good friends as well as relatives, had us all over. It was so nice to have my brother and his family meet *my* family. Well, not my mother, because she passed away in 2001, so Sharon and Ray were my closest family.

Our neighbors, the Susdorfs, came over for dinner one night and they invited all of us to swim in their pool anytime we wanted. Eszter and Ramona were delighted. They love the sun and the water so we availed ourselves of their generous offer several times.

We played cards a lot. Invited my friend Mary over as she loved to play cards too, and she fit right in. We were as close as sisters, but who knew I had a birth sister somewhere, so Mary became my American sister.

Ann was able to get home to La Crosse from her job in Minneapolis several times. I was so happy to again have the two first cousins be together.

And suddenly the trip was over. I was pretty exhausted. We decided that it would be more comfortable if I drove them back to Chicago to catch the plane, because five packed in the car at the beginning of the trip was kind of smushed. I know they thought I was racing away after I dropped them off but I had to get back home before it got too dark and late, and it was another four and half hours to drive back. They had a safe flight home and I slept for a week after they left.

2003 started out with us going to Arizona for three months, January through March. We spoke to Dieter, Eszter, and Ramona at Easter time.

Easter, like Christmas, is a big family time in Germany. We had stopped getting together with Ann at Easter because it was too little time to fly so far. We learned Helga had been in the hospital with bladder cancer. Surgery held it off temporarily. Detti was doing pretty well. Klaus loved calling me anytime, day or night. He would sing, tell me jokes, and he'd laugh and laugh. He had such infectious good humor. Over the years I grew to love him very much.

I practiced my German on our friends from Germany when we would meet them for dinner in Green Valley. The husband said that I was perfect, but I'm sure he was just being polite. I played German tutorial CDs in the car all the time, listened to German vocabulary tapes while I walked in the pool, and tried to keep up with my expensive but little used Rosetta Stone program. It all boiled down to the two years of German I had in high school with Sister Laurinda. She was a tyrant. Over and over she drilled us in grammar and vocabulary—and it stuck. Poor woman, I gave her a rough time in her class. Little did I know how much I would appreciate her discipline regime later in life.

Ramona emailed about her classes and about Dieter's garden house, and about her lack of interviews in Berlin. She was having a hard time finding a job and she really wanted to stay close to home. Helga had cataracts in both eyes removed. Detti, drinking again, was still having problems with his health.

Ramona wrote in April that her *"mum and dad are as often as possible in the weekend house….and of course dad has already started his fishing season. I can't imagine how someone can spend hours and hours with staring on one spot on the water. No good news on the job front, not even an interview. Helga was in the hospital for surgery. They found something on her bladder and removed it. She is in Poland over Easter. Take care. Love, Ramona"*

I'd like to write about Mary and Mark Spettel a bit. I know I talk about how out of date they were, how much older than my friends' parents they were, and how strict they seemed to me. And all of that is true. But, they loved with open hearts that were filled with fear that I might get hurt, either physically or emotionally. My mother was not as "warm and fuzzy" as my dad. She was the "buck up, it'll be fine" person. My dad was the type of parent that cried when he saw my scraped knee.

Throughout the years I spent with them, my father was always the consummate gentleman. At his funeral, and in the many letters of condolence we received, every person mentioned how much they respected him. He was generous to a fault with the church, with charities, with my mother, and with me. Anything that anyone needed, my dad tried to provide it for them. Only after his death did I find out how many people owed their businesses or houses to him, as he had loaned them money when they needed it.

He was a hard worker, honest to a fault, and in an era of having to save your own money for your own retirement, he did quite well. Both he and my mother never lived ostentatiously. They drove a moderate car, they lived in a moderate house, and they never, ever spoke of how much money they had. I remember a friend telling me once in grade school that her dad had told her that our house was worth $50,000. I was shocked, as that seemed like a great deal of money to me. I went home and told my dad. He just smiled and said, "Well, let him think what he wants." I never knew if that meant it was worth more or less.

Mark planned to become a lawyer. My mother worked as a secretary for a law firm when they were first married. She wanted him to be a lawyer, as that would be prestigious in her mind. But, fate stepped in and brought Mark back to La Crosse when his father died. Mark needed to take over the family business—a grocery store. Mark had an older brother, Frank, who had made his career in the army and therefore could not help out with the store. Eventually, Mark and Mary sold the grocery business and Mark worked for a number of years for a local office supply company.

From that experience, he ventured out on his own to start Spettel Office Company. His former employer, as a gift, gave him the franchise for one of the typewriter companies that was not doing all that well—Smith-Corona. Years later, it was one of my dad's best-selling typewriters. Mother and Dad said they agonized over what to purchase to fill the shelves of the store. Smith-Corona required that they have both a storefront and $1000 worth of merchandise on the shelves. When my dad retired in 1968, he was ordering $1000 worth of pencils at a time.

They were good people and very well-respected in the community. While my dad was a smiling, friendly, warm man, my mother had some issues. She was always worried. What would the neighbors think? Did her friends expect her to do this or that? Was the pastor happy with their donation? This paranoia escalated over the years and made for some difficult times before she finally needed to go into a nursing home at 92. She lived a full life. She passed away at 98. I cried for her, of course, but knew that she was already in Heaven advising God on the mistakes He'd made that day.

My parents were married 67 years and loved each other throughout every one of them. Of course, my dad, being such a nice man, let her have her way in everything, and he treated her like a queen. He would have been Sir Galahad in another era, laying his cloak down for his lady to walk across a puddle. He actually went out to the detached garage and started her car for her, backed it out of the garage, and if it was raining, would walk her out to the car holding an umbrella over her head. If it was icy, he was holding her arm to support her so she wouldn't fall. He was the type of man that was only happy if the people he loved were happy.

He wore his heart on his sleeve and I never doubted that he loved me. I don't think I appreciated Mary's love for me until I had a child of my own. Mary's love translated into worry and frustration at the lack of perfection in raising a living being, but it was the only way she knew—and she did try.

We had happy times, of course we did, and they were wonderful people who tried to be wonderful parents. I wish now that I had tried harder to let them know I appreciated all they did for me. I hope that in a small way I lived up to their expectations.

Dad was 80 when our daughter was born, but they were such health nuts and so determined to be active and well that they were a very functional part of her life. They kept her for two and a half weeks when Jim and I went to Europe in 1981 and Ann was only three. They were 83 and 79 at the time. What energy they had! It was amazing. Ann was

12 when my dad passed away. It was hard on her. She loved him, and he loved her so very much. Luckily, she had Jim's dad as a grandpa, who was a little younger and no less committed to a healthy lifestyle. Ann was out of college when my mother passed away. That made it easier for her and for us, too. The parents that I worried so much would die young and leave me with who-knows-whom lived well beyond my fears.

I never had any grandparents in my life. I think it's a special connection that I missed out on. My husband and I are determined that our grandson will know us, so we fly out to see him four or five times a year and they come to Green Valley once a year. It's not enough, will never be enough, but it is what it is. The easiest life is one of acceptance.

Chapter Forty-Four

2003—Our Trip To Germany

In 2003, Jim and I flew to Germany for two weeks. We arrived in Frankfurt-on-Main and checked in at the Hotel Frankenhof. Klaus assured us it was only a few blocks from his apartment. After getting settled, we walked to Klaus' but he was not home. We left a note on the door and went back to our room and slept for three hours, only waking up to the sound of knocking at our door. It was Klaus.

We were so tired. We decided to spend time with Klaus the next day. We slept more, and later ate quietly near our hotel. We went to Klaus' the next day at 11:00. We met his common-law wife, Irene, and one of his sons, Erhard. After lunch at Klaus' apartment, Klaus, Jim, and I got into a rental and drove around Frankfurt. I let my brother sit in the front so he could direct us, but mostly he just moaned and groaned because he thought Jim was driving too fast. Klaus probably had not driven a car in 25 years. Being around Klaus for so many hours was a little difficult. He probably would have been labeled ADHD if that was a thing when he was young.

He constantly found opportunities to clown around and he prattled continually. And he complained! Oh boy, did he complain. He couldn't see, he couldn't breathe, and he couldn't *pay*. Near the end of the day we told him we were tired and needed to go to our room to rest. We took him home and drove right back to the *Altstadt* (old city) to do our own sightseeing. Later we went to Klaus' for a dinner of wieners, potato salad, meat salad, dark bread, and water. The next day Jim and I took a Grey Line tour of Frankfurt. After the tour we walked back to our hotel—about two and a half miles. In the evening we picked up Klaus and drove to their Garden House where Klaus wanted to show off his *Grillmeister* skills.

Irene had biked the three miles to get there. And she would ride her bike home again in the dark. When we arrived, Irene had the patio decorated and tables set. First, before dinner, we had plum kugel with whipping cream. Erhard was there with his girlfriend, Ennis. She spoke English very well and we learned she was a Communist. Later in the evening we had steaks, sausage, and zucchini/tomato/mozzarella salad. Erhard was 44 at the time. His brother, Gerald, was 43, and his younger brother, also named Dieter, was 42.

Erhard always knew he had two younger brothers that had been given up for adoption. Klaus and Irene had been together for 45 years. Irene was still working part-time as a cleaning lady. I found out that Irene owned the garden house by herself. Klaus was not even allowed to have a key. *Poor Klaus, no one seemed to respect him, but they accepted him.*

After heartfelt goodbyes, we took Klaus back to his apartment and drove on to Kronach the next day to visit people we had met in Green Valley through mutual friends. We stayed in a *Pension* in the foothills of the mountains. It was beautiful and quaint—very Heidiesque. That evening our friends grilled brats for us at their house, a sauerkraut concoction, bread that Christa had made, and later a raspberry and crème in a meringue for dessert. The following day Wolfgang drove Jim and I all around the area in his brand new Mercedes. It was nice to have a native show us around, but it was not relaxing driving with Wolfgang. He drove like a maniac.

We ate dinner on the patio at the Gasthaus Dinkel. It was freezing, and I was not loving that too much. Wolfgang had Jim drive the car back to Kronach because he'd had several beers. In Germany if you get caught drinking and driving the fine was in accordance with your income. Since he owned a very lucrative business, he didn't want to take any chances. The second day he took us to one of the companies he owned. They made dashboards for Mercedes-Benz. More sightseeing to Bayreuth.

We ate *Lieberkasse* sandwiches for lunch and meat sticks, but they tasted terrible. That night we ate at a Greek restaurant. It was not something I wanted to do. I wanted to enjoy mostly German food. I thought I'd be safe ordering shrimp, but I was wrong. The little buggers were served with their heads on. I didn't want to make waves (or throw up) so I closed my eyes and cut off the heads and then ate the rest of it. Yuck again.

After dinner we went back to their house for dessert on the patio. Have they heard of eating inside where it's nice and warm? Jim drove Wolfgang's Mercedes again because Wolfgang wanted to enjoy a couple drinks. Jim still talks about driving through the *extremely narrow* walled streets of Kronach from the restaurant to their house.

From there we spent a week in Berlin visiting with my brothers and my sister. Jim and I stayed in a small studio apartment-type hotel about six blocks from Dieter's apartment. It was clean and quite nice, but there were no restaurants nearby.

The first night we ate at Dieter's and Eszter's apartment—noodle soup, stuffed cabbage, chicken, kohlrabi, and french fries. That was followed by two desserts and fresh fruit—pears from their garden and apple kuchen with apples also from their garden. We all strolled along the River Spree after dinner. I wanted to recreate some of my first visit for Jim. Back at their apartment we had a little gift exchange, then Jim and I walked back to our apartment/hotel.

The next morning Jim and I walked to a place where we could get enough cash to pay for our condo/hotel because we found out they did not take credit cards. It was 345 Euros for five nights. It was raining later, but we all went to see the Tegal area where Dieter grew up. I was able to show Jim where my grandmother lived. Then we drove to Helga's new apartment, which had an elevator. It was kind of like an independent care facility.

Her apartment was pretty nice. It had a balcony, of course. Dieter and Eszter left the two of us there for lunch with Helga and came back later to get us. During that time we walked the grounds, played some cards, and sat and sat and sat and sat. We made arrangements to all go to the garden house with Ramona and Detti. I couldn't wait to show Jim the garden house. We spent a lovely afternoon and evening there and laughed and told stories and made memories.

The next day Jim and I took a 14-stop bus tour. We shopped along the Ku'dam, went to the famous department store, the KaDeWe, and ate lunch at a Movenpik with a window table and a great view of the street. Later that afternoon we all went to Detti's apartment to visit.

It was the first time I had seen it. He was obviously feeling much better and was very hospitable. His significant other, Rosie, was very nice, but seemed like she had some dementia. Detti gave me an elephant from his collection. We both collected elephants. Then it was back to Dieter's for dinner. It was superb as usual. Eszter was still the wonderful cook I remembered from the first trip. We all played Uno afterwards. Jim won.

In the morning, Jim and I walked all around Pottsdam Platz and then on to Checkpoint Charlie and then back to the apartment to rest. We went over to Dieter's so he could drive us to see places of interest regarding my life—where I was born, where I would have been baptized, and the cemeteries where relatives were buried. I wanted Jim to see all that Dieter had shown me on my first trip.

Dieter told me something new. Gerhard never wanted any of his children to marry someone who already had children because they would not be blood relatives. *Could this be why he didn't want to take responsibility for me? He didn't think I was his blood?* Dieter wanted to show Jim the Mercedes Benz dealership. Eszter made schnitzel, fried eggplant, mashed potatoes, and cucumber salad. We watched the video Dieter had made of his trip to La Crosse, played cards again, and said our goodbyes.

We ended our trip to Germany by driving to Hamburg to visit a couple that I had only met online through Miriam, the foreign exchange student who helped me with translating when Helga visited Wisconsin. This couple was her aunt and uncle, Karin and Jac. I had been communicating with Karin for several months and we had become friends. When Karin found out we were going to be so close to Hamburg, she asked us to visit. At first it seemed odd to me, to visit someone we never met, but we decided that it would be a great way to see more of Germany, and it's always so nice to have native speakers show you around.

Miriam, their niece, surprised us by being there when we arrived. She had driven four and half hours to see us and had to leave at 6:30 to go back. After getting acquainted with Karin and Jac and renewing our acquaintanceship with Miriam, we checked in to our hotel, which was expensive but very lovely. They had told us when we were planning the trip that we were welcome to stay with them, but Jim and I don't really like staying with people. The hotel they found for us, near their house, was exquisite. They took us sightseeing and then back to their home for a wonderful dinner followed by a delicious dessert trifle.

The next day they took us to see the wharf. Wow, what a huge place that was. We found out Hamburg has more bridges (2300 of them) than Venice. For dinner we ate at a gourmet restaurant in Pinneberg, the suburb where they lived, where they insisted on paying.

We walked the city the next day with Karin and Jac as our guides. We ate at a little café, shopped at expensive shops, and took a boat tour of the harbor. Then we got in a cab and they took us to the "sex center" of the city. Prostitution is legal in Germany. There is a street in Hamburg where only men can walk and Jac insisted that Jim walk it with him. We "girls" had to stand at the end of the street, not even allowed to see the street in the distance because it was walled up at each end with actual guards to allow only men in.

Karin rolled her eyes several times, and said it was a tourist attraction. After that we all walked down Reeperbahn, the street where all the peepshows and exotic dancers were. The whole area is called St. Pauli. Later we ate at a steakhouse. It was the best meal of my whole trip.

We checked out and tried to pay for our room the next morning before we left to drive back to Frankfurt, but found out that Jac and Karin had paid for it already. We were shocked. We tried to get the clerk to let us pay, but she wouldn't. We had to wait until we got back to America to thank them. It was really very generous of strangers to do that. And yes, they had money—he was owner of the third largest bakery in Germany, but still, it was so unexpected. I told them that they would always be welcome to visit us, and they did, both in Minnesota and in Arizona. We continue to this day to write several times a year.

Interesting aside: Germany lets homeless people own dogs and it pays for the care of the dogs because it makes the homeless feel good about life. Also, you can live in any of the European Union states and not give up your citizenship. Germany is one of the cheaper places to visit for food and lodging, but petrol is very expensive. All the lights in all the hallways in all the public buildings and hotels are on timers to save electricity. It was very scary to get off the elevator in your hotel and hurry to try to trigger the first light sensors so you could find your way to your room.

Jim and I drove back to Frankfurt from Hamburg. We had to be at the airport very early the next day and we were exhausted after two weeks of traveling and sightseeing and visiting.

I was so happy that I could show Jim my Germany, my Berlin.

Taking time out for an ice cream treat in Frankfurt.

Klaus entertained us VERY informally.

Detti's apartment was more like a museum.

Das Grillmeister

Irene, Klaus' 'wife' and I getting to know each other.

Chapter Forty-Five

2004–2006 The Sands of Time

In September we were dealing with Jim's dad, Hank's, decline. He was getting weaker and losing weight. We had Meals on Wheels delivered to him every day and also got an in-home helper. Jim, his sister Karen, his sister Susan, or I went to visit him every day to make sure he was eating properly and to help him with clothes, meals, and shopping. It was hard on the three siblings that were living so far away. David, the oldest boy lived in Colorado, and Nancy, the oldest girl, lived in Maryland. JoAnn, the second to the youngest girl, lived in New Hampshire. They would visit, call, write, and send gifts, and that took some pressure off those of us near Hank.

Dieter and I wrote back and forth every few weeks. He talked about the garden house and the weather and Ramona being in Budapest for her new job at a bank. He was glad that I could understand his emails. He wrote, *"If there are mistakes in my letter, I beg pardon for them, but I have to find out many words in my dictionary and my grammar is not the best anymore. But, I know, that you understand all I mean, you are my other left slipper, if you don't understand me, who else?"*

In almost every email I asked Dieter and Eszter to come again to visit us in The States, either to Minnesota or Arizona. It never worked out. I wrote and told Dieter that I was sewing curtains for our new house. He wrote back saying that our grandfather on Gerhard's side was a master tailor. Any sewing that needed to be done in their house growing up was done by Gerhard, not Erika. He proudly admitted that he, Dieter, was the one who did all the sewing on the sewing machine in their household now.

In October Ramona told me that Detti was in the hospital again. She said he was not following his diet and he was drinking too much. Drinking too much was his constant problem. Klaus was complaining to Dieter that he had no money. Ramona said the economy was so bad.

That year I joined a German women's luncheon group. It was mostly comprised of ladies from all parts of Germany and they were very accepting of me. However, the rule was that we only spoke German during the time we were together. It was too difficult for me to keep up, and I dropped out.

In April we flew with Ann to Berkeley to find an apartment for graduate school. We had to be gone over Helga's birthday, so I wrote and asked Ramona to communicate that news to her.

I was getting ready to retire after sixteen years at the university. We had bought property in Minnesota only a few feet from the banks of the Mississippi River and were getting ready to build a house. Our plan was to live six months in the Midwest and six months in the Southwest. We would get a second car for each house and drive a car back and forth with cats, clothes, and computers.

We moved into our river house at the end of July 2004. Ann had quit her job because she was going to go to graduate school at UC–Berkeley, so she moved out of her apartment and back home with us only the week before our move. First, we had to put her stuff in our Wisconsin house and then had it moved along with everything else to the Minnesota house and then in a few weeks we had to repack Ann's items for her two-year stay in California. That was a crazy busy time.

We moved Ann to Berkeley in the fall and, on our way home from California, we stopped in Salt Lake City to meet my nephew, Gerald, and his family. He was one of three brothers and one of the two sons that my brother Klaus had given up for adoption. Gerald was adopted by a military man and his wife. It was a private adoption. Unfortunately, Klaus also gave up another son for adoption and that son was raised in an orphanage. Gerald said his adoptive parents would have been thrilled to raise both of the boys together if they had only known.

We went to Arizona in early November of 2004. It is a 27-hour drive. We always did it in one night so we could be in the warm weather sooner. A few weeks later we drove from Arizona to Berkeley to be with Ann for Thanksgiving. I sent out an early Christmas greeting telling people that we'd love to see them in Arizona, but our new motto was: one visit, one week. We were feeling a little overwhelmed by visitors. Hank was always welcome to visit for as long as he wanted, but he had slowed down on traveling.

I really wanted Dieter, Eszter, and Ramona to visit us, but I worried that in our small house we would drive each other nuts. I offered to have them stay in our house for one week, and then I'd find a place for them to stay for a couple more weeks. It wasn't worth their time and money if they didn't come for at least three weeks or more. Unfortunately, they were not able to make a trip to the States that year. I sent a Christmas letter to Ramona and she translated it for my siblings. I asked Helga to bring her friend who spoke English if she wished to come visit us again. I know they all thought I was being inhospitable, but our house in Arizona is not large.

For a Christmas present in 2004 Ann signed me up with a personal trainer at the local gym. Jim was faithful in going to the gym every single day, me not so much. I went when I wasn't too busy getting ready to go out for lunch with friends. I also got involved in the computer club, Newcomer's Club, studied Native American history, and we joined a couples' golf group..

In February of 2005, my friend, Mary, came to visit. She wanted to see my house and the Southwest. It was fun to show her my life down here. She and I retired at the same time, and I was hoping I could convince her to come to Green Valley for a month or more each year.

Ramona wrote about her new job in Budapest. It was far from her mom and dad but within the heart of her mom's extended family. Ramona was very familiar with the city and spoke the language fluently. We learned that Detti was in the hospital again and that he was not expected to live. *I was shocked. How could that be? And I thought again how lucky I was that I found them when I did.* Then, right on top of that news, Helga had to be rushed to the hospital because of more issues with her bladder. *Could I be losing two of my siblings?"*

By early April, Detti had died. I had a hard time wrapping my brain around that because he was so far away and I knew so little about what had happened. He would be cremated and buried in the same cemetery as our mother and father, but not in their plot. His would be a small square plaque with a number on it. That was all. It would take four weeks until the funeral because the state needed to find all the relatives. Detti did not leave a will.

Dieter told me that Detti married his first wife when he was 17 and she was 16. They had to get special permission from their parents. It lasted four years and produced two boys. Then another marriage and a daughter. A third marriage and another daughter. This marriage lasted three years. Detti lost all connection to his first 4 children, but in 1974 he married his fourth wife, Karin. She had four children by her first marriage and Detti had four children. They had one together—a boy named Ronald. Detti's relationship with his youngest son only lasted through the 10 years that Detti was married to Ronald's mother.

Ann was settled and doing well at Berkeley. She had friends and was enjoying her social life and her studies. She was shocked at how expensive housing was in California and talked about possibly moving to Seattle after she graduated.

Ramona emailed about her classes. I emailed about our move to Minnesota, she about Dieter's garden house. Helga had cataracts in both eyes removed and Klaus was complaining because he didn't have enough money.

It was during this year that I discovered that I liked writing. I joined a group called "Write Your Life" in Green Valley and I wrote about finding my birth family. The class was fascinated by my tale and I was happy to share it. I belonged to that group for several years, writing my birth family story chapter by chapter.

From there I branched out to a writer's group who shared their words/work for peer critique. We all wrote different things, but it was interesting and challenging. I realized that writing a whole, long book was hard to focus on, so I started writing short little stories about something funny in my present or past life. They were what I thought of as "one time reads" and I wrote them just for fun for my critique group. The group members laughed at what I wrote, and I would file the short story away never expecting to look at it again. That is, until an acquaintance back in Minnesota, Diana Hammell, who was an editor for the local newspaper, asked me if she could print a photo I had shared by email. I agreed, of course, and I wrote a funny little story to go with the photo. That's when my new "career" as a humor columnist began. Luckily I had all those former short stories. I polished them off a bit and used them for my weekly columns; however, eventually I had to start writing new ones and changed to writing only once a month.

I found a neighbor (Kris Campestrini) in Green Valley who spoke German. For a year she translated the letters I wrote to Helga into German. I really wanted Helga to know what I was feeling, but it was impossible to express myself well enough in German. Helga was not doing well health-wise. This was hard to deal with after so much happiness at the beginning of our family reunion.

Detti was buried on May 25, 2005; a sad day for my siblings. Klaus was not there, nor was I, nor were any of Detti's five children. The woman he lived with, Rosie, was there as was her daughter (to drive her). And of course, faithful Helga was there with him till the end, and Dieter and Eszter. But that was it. That is what his life came down to—five people to stand by his urn at the end. And so he was gone. I had shared the same space with him perhaps five or six times. No more chances to catch up, no more chances to learn more about him, no more chances to grow old together. At least he was buried near Mama and Papa. Now I worried about Helga because she had had two bladder surgeries.

Klaus called Jim at the end of May to sing Happy Birthday. He stayed up till 1:00 a.m. his time, but Jim wasn't even home. I loved hearing from him always. Though he was jolly and good-hearted, he always said he was not feeling well, or that his eyes were getting worse (cataracts), or that he couldn't ride his bike (they didn't have a car) to the garden house anymore. I can't imagine overweight Klaus riding his bike there, anyway. It was miles away and along busy roads. I'm sure Irene was happy to go (ride her bike) there and have some time to herself while Klaus stayed at home in their apartment.

Dieter and Eszter got an email account and a computer because of Ramona living in Hungary. That was convenient for me, too. I could write to Dieter and he would write back. His English, always improving, was very understandable.

Gerald, my nephew from Utah, was able to go to Germany on a business trip and visit his birth mother and father. Unfortunately, during this trip to see his birth parents, his adoptive mother died and he had to cut his trip short.

This would be the first Christmas for Klaus, Helga and Dieter without their brother, Detti.

"Alas," Dieter wrote, *"It is very sad, he, the youngest of us four here, had to go first. At the other side, we got back our little sister after so many years of unsuspecting about your existence, and we are very happy about your being, and we love you."*

Every year on Christmas day, since we found each other, we talked on the phone. Ramona and I talked for the most part, and Dieter listened on the speaker phone, but Dieter and I would chat for a while. I did not talk to Helga much on the phone. It was impossible with her not speaking any English.

Dieter always had fun calling me "little sister" even though I was several inches taller than him, and me calling him "big brother" while I stood on my tiptoes and looked down on the top of his head with a grin.

In the winter of 2006, Jim had a heart attack. It was so unexpected. If anyone would be having a heart attack, it should have been me, not the guy who exercised faithfully every day. One artery was 100 percent blocked. The others were all perfect. They put in a stent and he was out of the hospital in a few days. We were in La Vegas (a planned trip) a week later.

In May 2006, Ann was getting ready to graduate from Berkeley with a graduate degree in Public Policy and was busy looking for employment in Washington DC. We helped her move there right after graduation. She had flown to Arizona from California that spring break and stayed a week. It was her first time visiting Arizona in the spring when the flowers were all blooming and the weather was consistent. Jim continued to improve from his unexpected heart attack. We were making plans to return to Wisconsin early because he needed to see a specialist for a follow-up appointment and our insurance (an HMO) was only good for Wisconsin. Plus, we would be heading out by car for Ann's graduation and then would be packing up a U-Haul to drive cross-country to DC.

Ann would fly to DC and we would all stay at Jim's sister Nancy's house in Maryland. We wanted to help Ann find an apartment and help her get settled before we could return to the Midwest and start our summer. One cat had died right before we left for California and the other one was missing us, I was sure.

On December 28, 2006, Jim wrote an email to Dieter. Dieter had sent us a CD for Christmas where he had sung all the songs himself, with titles from Elvis and Nat King Cole and lots of oldies but goodies. Jim wrote,

"Dieter, you are in big trouble with our government. The CD was hand-delivered to us by two CIA agents because it was intercepted by our Homeland Security Agency. They checked for codes and hidden messages. That is why it

took so long for it to get to us. When they listened to it, they passed it on to President Bush! Everyone who listened to it thought it was Elvis! Now they want to know if Elvis is still alive and who sent us this CD. I told them I paid $100,000 for this original. So, Dieter, when you come to visit us you will also have to grow more hair and long sideburns. I will keep you informed if our government starts to look for you. Have a nice day but keep looking over your shoulder, Jim."

Luckily, Dieter and Ramona already understood Jim's sense of humor.

Ann's graduation from UC-Berkeley with a degree in Public Policy

Meeting my nephew, Gerald, and his family in Utah. I was shocked
by how much alike we looked.

Chapter Forty–Six

2006–2015 Time Passes So Quickly

It was just after the New Year's festivities that I wrote to my brother. My niece was working in Budapest and I'd sent her a present that never arrived. The mail was notoriously inefficient in Hungary. Items in letters and packages were often stolen. I talked about the nice weather in Arizona, that Jim's knee was not so great but we still golfed when we could, and that I understood if Helga didn't think she could make such a long trip again to visit me. *Secretly I was glad that was the case. Another visit from her and I would have gone nuts.*

Dieter wrote of visiting Helga and having lunch. She made *"asparagus and boiled potatoes and fried cutlets as big as toilet-seat lids."* While he was there Klaus called and Helga told him that she didn't want to talk to him again until he had gone through with his cataract operation as she was sick of listening to him moan and groan about not being able to see.

Emails continued. We discussed weather and trips and dieting. We all talked about dieting a lot because we all needed to do it. Dieter has been riding his bike but couldn't do that in the winter. I was going to the rec center and swimming.

In February, Dieter wrote a little bit more about Mama and Papa. It was in response to a comment he had made about Mama being afraid of doctors, and I asked about that. He said, *"Erika very feared from the doctors and I remember, finally she went to the doctors when she got more and more pain from the cancer. I also remember that Papa was very angry about it and then he sent Mama ultimately energetically to the doctors. But, it was too late for a good end. Papa was not ill often in his life and he was not afraid from the doctors. But he very fighted against the pain at the end of his life. I remember, till his birthday in October of 1977, he drived his car every day. But then he had terrible pain yet, took drugs against the pain and beared it till Mamas' birthday to celebrate yet at home. In the late evening, when all the birthday guests went home, he said to Mama, 'Now you have to take me to the hospital. I can't bear the dreadful pain anymore.' They took him to the hospital the night of Mama's birthday. He did not come home again and stayed in the hospital till his end of life on 27. Dec. 1977."*

Later Dieter wrote these lines, *"As you see, we always have to wish the best health to each other, fortune and money are nothing if you aren't in a good health, isn't it?"* He signed it: *"Your other left slipper, your brother from over the ocean, but in the reverse direction."*

Helga was taking short trips to England and Spain. I was glad for her to get away from Berlin when she could. Dieter and Eszter would go to Budapest for a month and see Ramona before taking a vacation to Croatia by the Adriatic Sea. *"We are glad to hear the Jim is well and I would say he is the old Jim again, like we know him."*

Ramona wrote and said she and her parents had vacationed for two weeks in Tunisia. She said they came home "brown." The Germans love the sun and the warmth of southern climates.

On my 58th birthday, all my family called, but I missed each call because we had gone to a friend's cottage. I called Helga back, but understood almost nothing of what she said. She spoke too fast. Klaus called me and shared that he had finally had both eyes operated on. One was perfect but the other was not, so he would have to go back again in a month. We were all (Germany and America) experiencing hot weather, which seemed to have covered the globe. Miriam's aunt and uncle, Karin and Jac from Hanover, were in the Midwest and would be coming to visit us for three nights in August. We were very excited to pay them back for their generosity when we visited them.

Ann called from Washington DC in August of 2006 and said, "Mom, let's go to Germany right now. I don't have a job yet—it's now or never. I want to meet Helga and Klaus and see all the places you told me about when you visited in 2000 and 2003." At first I just laughed at her suggestion, as there had been a lot of terrorist activity in airports recently. Then I thought of how much I wanted Ann to meet her Aunt Helga and Uncle Klaus. Detti had already passed away and she would never meet him. So, I planned our whole trip in three days. By the following Friday I was flying to DC where I would stay one night with Ann before we flew to Frankfurt for the first leg of our journey—visiting Klaus and his family.

Helga was not thrilled that we were coming at that particular time. She was planning a trip to Canada. She wanted us to come after her trip, but I knew Ann would probably have a job by then. Dieter and Eszter were planning to go to Budapest also, but Ann and I were staying in a hotel in downtown Berlin, so no one had to be put out by our staying with them. We arranged to stay a couple nights in Frankfurt first.

Ann got to experience her silly Uncle Klaus and also meet Irene and their son Erhard. It was nice for Ann to meet another first cousin. They had us over before going out to dinner; a tin of cookies and a warm soda were the appetizers. Typical Klaus said that at 5:45 we had reservations at 5:30 for a restaurant four blocks away. Sigh.

Coincidentally, the restaurant was in the hotel Jim and I had stayed in three years before when we had visited Klaus. I paid for the meal. We sat and talked for an hour and then decided to have dessert. I tried to pay for it, but Erhard insisted on paying, which was very sweet of him to do. Ann and I had gifts for them that we had brought from America.

After three days in Frankfurt we drove to Berlin. It took us six hours and it was a thrilling experience. Jim and I had rented a car when we were there in 2003, but he did all the driving. Now I was doing all the driving. *Yikes.* Ann was a good navigator, however. We just kept up with the traffic which was mostly going 100 MPH, I am pretty sure.

Ann and I stayed on the Kurfurstendam for five nights. It is the famous shopping street in Berlin. It was fun to have Ann be part of the experience. We did a lot of shopping and sightseeing, but not what we might have done if we'd had more time. Dieter and Eszter were warm and welcoming and it was wonderful to see them again. The first night they had us over for dinner. I was excited because I know what a good cook Eszter can be. She served soup, rolls, rumladen, meat balls, Wiener schnitzel, potatoes, and salad. For dessert there were two kinds of kuchen.

We stayed till 10 p.m. talking, but we were tired from the drive, so we headed back to the hotel early. We had breakfast on the Ku'dam (there was no restaurant in our hotel) and then back to Dieter's so he could show us Berlin. That night we had leftovers and Dieter showed Ann the video of my mother. The next day Ann and I did tourist sightseeing—things not on Dieter's list. We all ate that night at a typical German restaurant. Ann had sauerbraten with red cabbage and I had three meats, four vegetables, and a potato. You know, a "light" German meal. We had ice cream sundaes for dessert. We all went to see the Reichstag (the city hall) at night. At the top we were treated to a beautiful view of Berlin. Dieter and Eszter had never been to this building before. That's typical of all of us—we never seem to explore our very own backyards.

The next day we went to Helga's new apartment. She was cold and unfriendly. She served lunch. In the afternoon we drove to Dieter's garden house so Ann could see it. We had no time to actually enjoy a lengthy stay there this trip. Back to Helga's for supper. She had invited the son of someone she had dated years before to come to dinner, and she also invited her friend who spoke English so well. That helped the conversation go a little bit better, but Helga seemed determined to be aloof and standoffish. She barely spoke, and even her supper was minimal and unappetizing.

Her pseudo-son finally asked her if she had some bread. She did, and she had him go out into the kitchen to bring some in. It was an odd experience, and I suspected part of it stemmed from her anger that I had brought her clothes (that she had left at our house in Wisconsin) back to her when Jim and I had visited three years before. She had decided that she was not going to be friendly, and that was that. Despite that, I tried to plug along with some conversation. Mostly I was just hoping that the time to leave would come soon. *When I left, I hugged her and for some reason felt I would never see her again. And I was right.*

Ann and I drove to Heidelberg for two nights. I had remembered this quaint little town with fondness from when I was there in 1962 with Mary and Mark. Mary had relatives on her father's side who lived there back then, and I fell in love with it. I wanted Ann to see it. We got lost, and it took us longer than expected. It was a very modern, large hotel and that night we ate a wonderful barbecue meal. The next morning we walked to the *Altstadt* (old town) along cobbled streets and took the tram to the *Schloss* (castle) at the top of the mountain. After several hours touring the castle and grounds, we walked down all 400 steps back into the city. We had supper at an Italian restaurant along the route to our hotel. It was great, and we turned in early.

We returned to Frankfurt the next day and had an early dinner with Klaus and Erhard at a pizza place. We said our goodbyes before Ann and I drove to our hotel at the airport. As soon as we entered I knew it was the same hotel Jim and I had stayed in three years earlier. Only the name was different.

The next day we spent hours going through many security checkpoints. No one was allowed to even buy water in the airport, and that was before the advent of the 3-ounce bottles. We flew from Frankfurt to Philadelphia and then on to DC, arriving very late. We were hungry but too tired to care. We schlepped our luggage onto a shuttle from the airport, which took us to the metro, which took us to within a couple blocks of Ann's apartment. *Why in the world I didn't spring for a taxi I'll never know.* We were exhausted and went right to bed. The next day Ann went with me to the airport. We reversed our walk to the metro, then to the shuttle bus to take us to the airport. We said goodbye and I returned to Wisconsin. It was early September of 2006.

Ann found a job shortly afterward as a policy analyst for the Department of Agriculture. She would come to Arizona for Christmas, so we left earlier for Green Valley that year to get the house decorated.

Dieter wrote that it was the warmest day in Berlin in 100 years—63 degrees. He sent birthday wishes to Ann. *"Hallo Ann. Happy birthday to you. We wish all the best for your health, much luck for you and a good succeeding for your new job."*

I decorated for Christmas with an Arizona theme, including Mexican and Western ornaments. It was fun to start all over from scratch and finding new decorations. I was happy that the Southwest loved Christmas decorations, both inside and out. Each development in Green Valley tried to outdo the other with spectacular lights and decorations at their entrances. I thought I'd miss the Midwest's snowy Christmas, but I did not. It was perfect. Ann said she loved having Christmas dinner and then going to the pool afterward. My sister had yet another operation for bladder cancer.

Sadly, Jim's dad, Hank, passed away in early 2007. He lived 94 years, and that was wonderful. Most of his later life was very active. When the bus company added bike racks to their buses, Hank, 89 then, was the oldest La Crosse citizen to register to do that and he often rode the eight miles downtown on his bike and then he and his bike would get a bus ride home. The family decided to have a combined family reunion/memorial service in July in La Crosse. Jim comes from a family of four girls and two boys, and they all decided summer seemed like a better time for everyone to drive in or fly in. Dieter wrote, *"I think Hank will look down at this family reunion from the Kingdom of Heaven and he will rejoice about it."*

My German family had a lot of illness in the winter of 2007. Dieter had a blood clot go to his eye, but it healed. Ramona was sick a lot and missed some work. The snow and cold was getting everyone down. Surprisingly, Klaus the complainer was probably in the best health of them all. Dieter said they tried to help Helga with shopping and little things in the apartment but, *"Helga is not pleased with anything we do for her. You know her, she always knows all better than others."*

And then it was Thanksgiving again. Helga had been having some problems since October, but that was all Dieter could tell me. He was having difficulties of his own and needed a heart stent, like Jim. While Dieter was barely recuperating, Helga's neighbor called him and said she found Helga on the floor of her apartment, confused and weak. They got her to the hospital, but the doctors were not very hopeful about her prognosis. She could not speak and was in and out of consciousness. By early 2008 she was gone. Her funeral was February 1st. There were about 15 people in attendance. Erika's half-brother Heinz (I wish I could have met him on one of my trips) attended. I think it was very special for everyone to get together.

Dieter and Eszter closed down her apartment. They had trouble giving away her furniture. They were able to put a few things in their weekend house. Dieter was still having physical therapy for his heart problems, but by May he was doing very well and the doctors said he didn't have to return.

I had to email Dieter to wish him a Happy Birthday because I lost my voice and couldn't talk on the phone. Dieter wrote, *"I think you catched a cold during your short trip out of town with your girlfriends or you all shouted in a medley of voices of so many women are in common."* He has such a great sense of humor, my big brother. In early May we would leave Arizona for Minnesota. I missed my friends and the green grass and the Mississippi River.

Ramona got a new job in Koln (Cologne) Germany. Dieter wrote and told us, *"Her apartment is very clean, new built, sunny with balcony to the south, a build-in furniture-kitchen. It is on the first floor with parquet flooring and flagstones in the bathroom and kitchen. It has a living room, bedroom, very modern bathroom, corridor, a little room like a caboose to put away things you do not need every day."*

Like us, Ramona's parents made several trips to her new home to help her move in and get furnished and settled.

My 60th birthday and now only two siblings to call me. Ramona wrote and said she knew I would not be cooking for my birthday. She knew I liked to go out to eat; that I was lazy like Mama about cooking.

Ann had met someone special in 2008. His name was Erik Raven. He worked for the federal government. Ann had a new position by this time working for the DC city government. We got to meet her boyfriend several times on our trips out to see her. She went on vacation by herself to South America that summer. Jim and I were in a panic about it, but she was all grown up and very savvy so we just hoped all would go well. At Thanksgiving Ann and Erik traveled to London and Paris instead of spending the holiday with us, and I knew it was the end of an era.

They visited Erik's sister who lived in Paris and explored London where Erik had gone to graduate school at the London School of Economics. In a phenomenal coincidence, my niece, Ramona, was in London at the same time for her job. The three of them were able to meet for dinner one night and she and Ann could catch up.

Skype was becoming popular and in 2009 we tried to do some Skyping with Dieter, but it didn't work too well. Dieter's computer was older and didn't have a camera. They could see me and hear me, but I could only hear them. I called and talked to Klaus when I could, but I wished he had a computer. He didn't even have an answering machine for his phone. I think he was afraid of bill collectors because often he would not answer the phone at all.

I knew I could always call him very late at night his time because he was the ultimate night owl. We siblings were all having aches and pains. The price of getting older, I guess. Eszter had kidney stones and gallbladder issues. Dieter was having troubles with his eyes (cataracts), Jim had a bad shoulder, my knee was starting to give me problems, Eszter was having problems with her feet. I had a feeling that no one was going to come to America to visit us again, except maybe Ramona. Klaus would never be well enough to come and Dieter and Eszter were having too many medical issues to leave the country.

The year rolled over into 2010. Dieter said the *"snowflakes were as big as butterflies, falling down all over the town during the sunshining."* He had a successful operation on his eye and would have the second one done in the spring. And so the years passed with phone calls and emails and letters and pictures and Skype. We kept in contact, but the times in between grew longer. In some ways I was relieved that I only had to keep up with two brothers, and thank Heaven both spoke English. Dieter did well with his end of the conversation and Klaus knew enough to have a short conversation with me. Ann was busy. Ramona was busy. Jim and I enjoyed our two-home situation and increased our time in Arizona to six months.

We made up our minds that we would enjoy the moment. Wherever we were, that was home for the time we were there.

Ann married the love of her life, Erik Raven, one day before Jim and my 40th wedding anniversary—2012. They had a beautiful wedding in a gorgeous setting of a vineyard in Virginia. Because it was so far away from Wisconsin, we decided not to ask people to come all the way to Virginia and planned a second wedding reception back in La Crosse for a month later. The day of the wedding it threatened to rain all day, but held off till it was all over, which is what happened at our wedding 40 years before. We made a number of trips out to Washington DC to visit them, but, the trips really started in earnest in January of 2015 when our grandson Edward was born. He is the delight of us all—sweet and cute and smart and too big for his britches, but the love of our lives. Because of him, we now get to DC five times a year and they visit us once a year.

Ann and Erik's wedding day – at a vineyard in Virginia. Notice Erik holding Ann's "ruby red slippers (heels)"

Our adorable grandson with his Mommy and Daddy.

Ann and I visited Klaus, Irene, and their son Erhard in 2006.

Our grandson, Edward, arrived in 2015.

Chapter Forty–Seven

2010–2018 Life Moves On

I really wanted to title this *The Rest of the Story* (from Paul Harvey's radio show) but I thought his heirs might find out and sue me. I can't really say, "the end" either, because as long as I breathe, it's not "the end." I can say that Klaus, Dieter, Eszter, Ramona and all the other characters in my story lived each day, one after another, some good some bad, and we continued with our phone calls and sometimes a card or letter, but no one crossed the Atlantic for a visit. I felt very guilty about that but excused myself because of all our trips back and forth from Minnesota and Arizona, and then visits to Ann (then Ann and Erik, then Ann and Erik and our grandson, Edward).

We found time for a cruise or two, but nothing where I had to fly to get there. I hate flying, but I wanted to fly to Germany again. I didn't. Of course, I knew Klaus could never fly to the U.S. I can't imagine him even sitting that long. He would have gotten up, walked all around, told jokes, and ignored the seat belt sign. They would have had to land somewhere and remove him from the plane.

Eventually, we siblings started to miss the "exact" date of a birthday or a holiday and called a day before or a few days after. No more staying home by my phone waiting for calls from one of them. Now we would email (well, Ramona and Dieter and I did) and say when we would be around and set up our calling schedules, always keeping in the mind the eight-hour difference between us—or nine-hour) depending on if we were in Arizona or not.

Ann and Erik took Edward and flew to Berlin in 2016. Edward could fly for free, and Erik's sister, who lived first in Paris had just moved to Berlin with her twin daughters. Erik wanted to see her and the girls, and Ann could visit her cousin Ramona, Aunt Eszter, and Uncle Dieter. They all had a great time and Edward was a good traveler.

In May of 2016, Klaus' health deteriorated. It was even worse than his many previous health scares. I worried that he might not live much longer, but usually in the past he would rally and he'd call me and say he was home from the hospital and "being a good boy."

Dieter or Ramona had called me every few days to say how he was faring in the hospital. I had no way of checking on Klaus, but they could call Irene or Erhard to find out the latest info. Irene spoke no English. Erhard understood and spoke some, but he seemed hesitant to do so with me. Klaus remained very overweight and his lungs were not good. One day he went into the hospital and never came home. He died on June 1, 2016, in his early 80s.

And so, Klaus' three boys and two daughters lost their father. I'm not sure what happened to his daughters—they would be pretty old themselves at the time of his death. I believe that Klaus had no contact with them after he ran away from his family. He "ran" back home to Berlin, the place he had run away from, but our father told him to get back to Frankfurt and take care of his wife and children. So, no "prodigal son returns" story for Klaus. His three sons lost a dad that had never done much for them. He was not there for them physically and certainly not there for them financially.

He had given his two youngest sons away, and unfortunately, one did not get adopted—he was raised in an orphanage. My nephew in Utah was luckier; he was adopted by wonderful parents. But, for all his faults, Klaus had a sweet simplicity about him. He had never had anything, he never worked hard to get anything, but he had a smile (albeit missing several teeth) and a laugh that could light up the room. I'm glad he lived as long as he did, and I'm glad that I got to know him and have the years with him that I had.

Jim and I felt very lucky to have two beautiful homes. Being on the Mississippi River in the summer was glorious and avoiding the Midwest winters by spending our time in Arizona was marvelous.

However, it started to get to be a lot of work maintaining two houses. At least a month before we planned our departure from one house, we would have to eat all the food in the pantry and the refrigerator, we had to have "last dinners" with friends and neighbors, and we had to start putting things on the spare bed that we knew needed to go to our other home with us.

A day or two before we left, Jim covered up all the windows with weather shielding material (to keep it cool in Arizona and warm in Minnesota). The night before we left he unplugged the microwave, all the TVs, the oven, clocks, took batteries out of remote controls and wall clocks. It was such a long list of final things before leaving.

The morning of departure we would get up at 4 a.m., dress, pack the last of the items we needed, and then unplug the refrigerator, pack the cooler, hope we didn't forget anything, drive the car out of the garage, go back in and lock the garage doors, triple lock all the other doors and take one last look around because it would be six months before we returned. As we drove out of our neighborhood, I would wonder what the next six months would bring.

We had trained ourselves over the years to make the 27-hour, 1,700-mile trip in one night and even as we got older, we just couldn't seem to change that habit. Once we left one place we were in a hurry to get home to the other. It actually took me a long time to learn to let the "old" place fade from my mind and think of what was ahead for the next six months. Being brought up in Wisconsin, it took me a while to get used to desert plants, dust, brown, cactus, and high, bare mountains.

Then it happened. It was a slow process. First we discussed where we would live if we downsized. Minnesota, of course, we thought. We gave ourselves a timetable of about five years to get ready to sell. Then, each month that passed, we lessened the timetable. Maybe four years? Well, how about three years? Why are we waiting, let's do it in two years. Okay, let's give it one more year. And on the drive back to Minnesota that spring, it shifted to *that summer* we would put one house on the market. Two houses was one too many. But, which house to keep? I didn't really want to be in Minnesota in the snow and ice. We could come to Green Valley and rent, of course, but then we would be in someone else's house. I knew I would never like that.

We talked and talked about it, the pros and cons, back and forth, and suddenly, unexpectedly, the decision was made for us by Ann. She said that she and her husband would prefer to visit us in Arizona. The weather was consistent, it was much easier for her to fly in from DC, and there was so much for our grandson to explore. The three of us, then the four of us, now the five of us, celebrate Christmas in Arizona and have for many years now. Ann's approval was the deciding vote that helped us get off the fence. Arizona would be our full-time residence. We have not regretted it for one minute.

We were lucky and sold our house in Minnesota in three months. By November 1st we were headed back to Green Valley, to our new year-round home. It was made a lot easier by the fact that we had been coming here, to this house, this city, and this state for 18 years and that we had made lots of friends and become a part of the community.

During Christmas of 2017, I was speaking with Dieter, Ramona, and Eszter. I realized how much I missed then and wished that I hadn't let so many years pass without seeing them. My brother made a remark that stayed with me for days after we hung up. *"I wish I could see Green Valley, where you live, once before I die."* And that started the little seed that grew into a great idea and now has become a real plan. Dieter, Eszter, and Ramona will come to Green Valley next Easter. We have friends that will let us rent their house for a month because they will be back in La Crosse by then.

Ramona might not be able to stay the whole time, but Dieter and Eszter will. It will be great weather here in mid-April to mid-May and they will love it. *Why didn't I come up with this idea years ago?* Actually, now and then we did speak of them visiting, but there was always this or that getting in the way. My brother is nine years older than I am. I can't wait to see him again. Luckily, they love to fly—one major way Dieter and I are *not* alike.

I have to end my story here. Now you want to know the answer, don't you? What did I decide would have been better after having been given up for adoption two times, not growing up with siblings and birth parents, finding them and knowing what their lives were like, and what my life probably would have been like? Do I wish I had been raised with them, or were all the circumstances of my life what was meant to be and the best for me?

I can say this: although I now know who my family is, where my family was, how my family interacted with each other, and now that I know all the dynamics of my possible life in Germany, I cannot say that I wish I had not been given up for adoption.

I don't know how anyone can wish that their life had been completely different. I would have had less education, I would not have met Jim, I would not have had Ann and therefore my adorable grandson, Edward, and I would not be the person who is writing this book. I can't even imagine who I would be. That is too scary to even give a voice to: imagining how your life could have been different. The life I lived is the life I had. We all have to accept what the days of our lives were like—and I do.

Me with my nephew Erhard,
Klaus' son.

Detti, Helga, me,
Dieter in 2003.

Jim and I visiting
Klaus at his home
in Frankfurt in
2003.

Eszter, Ann, Edward, Ramona, and Dieter get together in Berlin.

Check out Bonnie's website at: www.BooksByBonnie.com